T0082722

I WAS A
FOSTER CARER

I WAS A FOSTER CARER

ADRIAN HAWKES

I WAS A FOSTER CARER

iUniverse books may be ordered through booksellers or by contacting:

iUniverse
1663 Liberty Drive
Bloomington, IN 47403
www.iuniverse.com
844-349-9409

ISBN: 978-1-5320-9171-1 (sc)
ISBN: 978-1-5320-9170-4 (e)

Library of Congress Control Number: 2021905148

Print information available on the last page.

iUniverse rev. date: 03/31/2021

Should you read this book? Yes! You certainly should! It's important. And I certainly say you should read it if you've ever thought of fostering and even if you've never thought of fostering. I give another great big yes if you're involved in social care. This is a book about my real-life experience of being a foster carer, written with the hope that it will encourage others to join the ranks of foster carers, notwithstanding the hard experiences and knowing there are rewarding times too. I really appreciate living in a country that has a social services system. However, as I often say, the worst enemy of better is very good. So, I do speak about the areas of our system that I believe need improving and changing.

Why do I think this book is unique? There are lots of books about what it's like to be fostered, and I think they should be read. However, I don't think there are many volumes about what it's like to be on the other side of the fence—in other words, books covering the personal experiences of being a foster carer. Hopefully, this will give you a taste of that. However, I have to add that I believe that no two foster carers—like the children they care for—will ever have the same experience.

Facts and figures: These are constantly in a state of upgrading and modifying. At the back of the book, I have put in the latest statistics at the time of writing. These can be checked on government websites for the latest updates. I can, however, confidently assert that they will increase year on year.

CONTENTS

FOREWORD

Adrian Hawkes has been a constant figure in my life for almost four decades. I had the privilege of attending a small independent school of which he was the principal. The school was a very positive environment. As kids, we were valued and believed in and told so on a regular basis. We were encouraged to go for our dreams and change the world for the better, if that was what we wanted to do.

When I tell people about the positive, constructive, morale-boosting experience of my school days, they are in absolute awe, because, for many, their experience of school was far removed from mine. So, thank you, Adrian, for being a great principal. But also, thank you for asking me to write this foreword to *I Was a Foster Carer.*

Adrian is a great orator and has the fantastic ability to tell stories that transfix all generations. If you've ever had the privilege of hearing him speak, you've definitely come away having laughed, as well as having been challenged and inspired.

Adrian is a can-do person, who sincerely believes that dreams are achievable. Throughout, *I Was a Foster Carer,* he writes about not settling for good when better can be achieved. He challenges people who say, "I can't," and asks them, "Why can't you? Have you tried to push that door?"

Adrian strives to be a force for good and to make changes for the better. In this book, he poses questions that challenge officialdom and some of social services' practises. In certain situations, Adrian objects to the tick-box system, where one size fits all, believing a more common- sense approach would be better.

I Was a Foster Carer is humorous, engaging, and informative. It's a good read, set in fifty-two bite-size chapters. It's an insightful bevy of stories, recounting Adrian's experiences as a foster carer, sharing his navigation through the foster care system, and briefly touching on the foster care system as it is now.

The statistics are startling, and many more foster carers are needed. Every twenty minutes, a child goes into care. And in 2018, the fostering service stated that it needed to recruit 6,800 foster families in the United Kingdom in the next twelve months.

I hope this book will inspire those who seek to foster to give that door a push. If you are considering becoming a foster carer, this book is an eye-opener to some of the realities of fostering—the sometimes - testing realities but also the incredibly rewarding ones too.

Ronke Coote, LLB (Hon.)
cofounder of Big Building Foundation

Ronke is a married mother of two. She is a solicitor and a secondary school "safeguarding governor" and sits in a legal capacity as a panel member for a foster care agency. She has a heart for social justice and would like nothing more than to see people living free from harm and abuse. Her main areas of work are with survivors of domestic violence and women who have been affected by the criminal justice system. Big Building Foundation is a social enterprise organisation that seeks to serve local communities. It was set up in 2014.

PREFACE

This is my eighth book. I guess this one is a bit of a specialist subject. I hope, however, that if you do not fit into what I have here called, "the specialist" section, you will still enjoy grappling with my stories. Here is a bagful of memories that are, by the way, all true. I have many more anecdotes of equal interest and fascination. I have, of course, changed all the names and occasionally amalgamated situations. But it's all real—all nonfiction.

I am hoping this book will be an influence on some. I have said more than once while sharing these accounts that I am glad that I live in a country that has social services. I travel a lot and have often been in places where there is no official or governmental protection for children. So, yes, I have seen children sleeping rough on the streets in the cold. And when I say "children", I don't mean teenagers. I mean young 3, 4, 5, and 6 year olds. I am glad that, here in the United Kingdom at least, those things should not happen. But occasionally …

I have also been to countries where children have died and been left on the rubbish dump. I have been present in situations where, when the local police were advised about a dead child being left on the rubbish tip, the response was, "Oh dear! We will remove the body." And that was the end of the story.

On one occasion, I was visiting a refugee camp in a certain country, and a lady literally shoved her baby into my arms. The whole thing happened so quickly that I took the baby reflexively. Ah! That really was the wrong thing to do. The distraught lady shouted at me,

"If you do not take my baby, he will die of starvation." I quickly put the baby back into her arms. But let me tell you that the picture of that mother and child still lives starkly in my mind's eye, and oh, how I wish it did not.

So, am I glad that we have social workers, social services, legislation, child protection, and the like? You bet I am. However, as I have also said in the book that follows, the worst enemy of better is very good. We cannot rest and say, "All is well! It's perfect!" It is not. Sometimes things are done in such a way that the system itself could be accused of being abusive to children. There are all sorts of reasons as to why that happens. Some are understandable. Some are because of wrong agendas. Some are because what is at the centre of our legislation regarding children—in other words, "children are at the centre"—is sometimes just words; and "my job" and/or "the good name of the agency", authority, money, and convenience also come into play. And if we were honest, often the child is moved from that central position of the priority, as well as from the legal position and status, to the margins of the entire process.

Frequently, our social workers have too large a caseload to do the job they want to do. In this area, I am extremely sympathetic. However, I hope that by writing this down and putting it out on the streets, I will persuade someone that change is needed in that area of social care.

Sometimes, we are not talking across agencies. We don't have those "joined-up services" that the government repeatedly says are going to happen. This leaves us with the Victoria Climbiés of this world. Victoria Climbié—2 November 1991 to 25 February 2000—was tortured and murdered by her great-aunt and her great-aunt's boyfriend, who were both convicted of murder and sentenced to life imprisonment. After Climbié's death, all the official parties connected to her care were widely criticised.

It gives us Rochdale and Rotherham. The Rotherham child sexual exploitation scandal consisted of organised child sexual abuse that occurred in the northern English town of Rotherham, South Yorkshire, from the late 1980s until the 2010s and the failure of local authorities to act on reports of the abuse throughout most of that period.

It gives us Baby P. Peter Connelly—initially known to the public as "Baby P"; "Child A"; and, later, "Baby Peter"—was a 17-month-old English boy who died in London in 2007 after suffering more than fifty injuries over an eight-month period, during which he was repeatedly seen by the Boroughs Children's Services and National Health Service (NHS).

Sometimes we—and it's the responsibility of all of us—just do not want to get involved, so terrible and shocking things happen.

Another reason for this book is that, for all its difficulties and pressures, foster caring is rewarding too. And I hope that *I Was a Foster Carer* will persuade someone to say, "I will do it! I will be a foster carer."

12 December 2017
Tottenham, North London

ACKNOWLEDGEMENTS

Thank you to all of you who have kindly read draft versions, commented, and corrected. You know who you are.

Thank you for all the social workers I currently work with for trying to go the extra mile. You do a great job.

Thank you to the publishers.

Thank you to my wife, who really does not like me writing books but somehow puts up with it.

Thank you to all those who have been fostered by my wife and me. We have been enriched by knowing you, and we hope your experience of living with us has benefitted you in the long haul of life.

INTRODUCTION

There are literally thousands of children in the United Kingdom who are desperately in need of love and care in a normal family home. Foster caring is a quite wonderful adventure, and I would like you to know how enriching it can be in any home—including those homes that already have their own birth families.

This book contains stories of my and my wife's fostering experiences. Some of it, I hope, you will find fun and interesting. I trust it will give you an insight into fostering and, maybe, hopefully, persuade you to be a foster carer. There is, it seems, always a shortage of foster carers.

I should say, of course, that I have not used the real names in my stories, preferring to maintain my foster children's anonymity. I have also amalgamated some situations to make my point. However, the situations themselves are all real experiences—and very, very real for my family.

It may seem, sometimes, that I am a little hard on social workers. Please don't misunderstand me, as I believe many social workers do a great job. Often, those working for local authorities in particular have far too big a caseload in my opinion. Also, sometimes it is very hard for social workers to make the right decisions concerning children in care. There are times when they are "damned if they do and damned if they don't!" However, and I don't know if it comes from their job insecurity or the public cases in which social workers have often been blamed, I find that many social workers are keener on protecting their job, their backs, and their positions than they are on protecting the child's best interests.

Again, I have to say that I can empathise and understand their plight. Often, because they are on the front line of dealing with what happens to a child when he or she is taken from his or her parents, there are times when, finally, social workers end up being blamed when things go wrong, even though they possibly gave it their deepest thought and activated what they believed was their best decision. This breeds a protective atmosphere, where the child ends up meeting the cost of it all by his or her life's outcomes. It is utterly unlike airline pilots, who, when they make a mistake, end up reporting themselves for a "no-fault inquiry", which has led to air travel being one of the safest industries.

I work in and visit countries where there are no social services to speak of. I am glad to have such a service for the protection of children in the country in which I live.

I work in and visit countries where there are no social services to speak of. I am glad to have such a service for the protection of children in the country in which I live. However, one of my favourite sayings is, **"The worst enemy of, "better" is, "very good.""** So, even if one believes what he or she has is very good, my plea is for people to—please—not allow the "very good" to stop us from seeing faults in the system and so prevent us from seeking to make what we have even better.

Once upon a time, I was the chair of a foster carer association for a local borough. I persuaded management that ongoing CPD (continuous professional development) should be a joint programme with social workers and foster carers. Management agreed and implemented an appropriate programme. However, the programme did not last very long. The social workers complained very loudly that they were professionally qualified as social workers, with degrees and the like, and should not have to do training with "unqualified", "nonprofessional" foster carers. I think they believed that being treated as if they were on par with foster carers was beneath their dignity.

Another time, I faced a similar issue with management. Foster carers complained to me that social workers would sit in planning meetings with children of 11 years old and upwards and say, in front of the children, "Your foster carer gets such and such an amount of money to look after you. You need to know that." The problem is that many younger children, never mind foster children, do not process costs very well at all. Most birth children think that lighting, heating, water, and living in a house are all freebies. They only discover the financial facts of life when they leave home. So, discussing the financial arrangements with a young child is not helpful to the placement. When I complained to the management about this practise, the senior manager told me, "If you knew how many times, I have told the social workers they must not do that, you would be amazed. However, I cannot act on your information unless you give me the social workers' names."

The foster carers, of course, did not want to get any social worker into trouble, so I could not pass that information on.

I have to say that, in my experience, there have been some great social workers, who have done a fantastic job. There were common threads in the work of these positive, influential workers. (1) They did not seem to feel insecure. (2) They often used a very common-sense approach towards the carers and the children. (3) They were willing to listen to a foster carer's perspective. (4) They also seemed to be aware that the foster carers were with the children 24/7. That is well worth remembering. Many of the very best social workers fostered children themselves. These people really understood the issues, the pressures, and what was appropriate to say, or not to say, in front of the children.

All in all, though, please remember that, as I write about my experiences, I do seriously appreciate the system. I am aware that some local authorities are looking at social pedagogy ways of working by learning from other countries - like Finland. In the Finnish system, when children are being placed, all - from the child to the foster carers to the social workers to the birth families - have an equal stake and say on what is done. At the moment in the British system, it seems to me that, as a foster carer, you are a lesser individual; and although you are responsible for the care of a child 24/7, you are considered not an expert or a professional. Often the carer's views concerning what is going on with the child are pushed to one side because, "You don't have a social work degree."

I did have one of the qualified social workers, who also fostered, working with us, though. She listened the best to us. A system that encouraged more social workers like her could make better short-term outcomes much more likely, as well as producing better ends, not creating an "us and them" kind of experience or an experience that puts others in the position of a lesser human being whose knowledge is irrelevant. All these things are reflective in the speech and attitude of everybody in the Finnish system.

What is pedagogy? Social pedagogy is a method of social work or working with children that allows all to have their say. The child, the foster carer, the social worker, and the management all have something to bring to the table, and each has his or her voice heard and respected.

Working within the foster care environment, I have experienced and overheard key workers talking with social workers. I once overheard a key worker on a phone call to a social worker. (A key worker is a trained member of staff allocated to individual clients working to ensure that the legalities and practicalities of "the care system" are properly being implemented. Sometimes key workers are qualified social workers, and occasionally they're qualified in other aspects of the "care system.") When I asked at the end of the call, "Are you OK?" she replied, "Yes, I am. But why do social workers think we are all idiots and know nothing? I don't have a social work degree, but I do have a degree, and I'm not stupid."

On another such occasion, I listened to a social worker talking to a key worker. The social worker was obviously belittling and negating the key worker's opinion, treating the key worker as a "stupid know-nothing". I was amused at the end of the conversation when the key worker turned to the social worker and said, "Well! Thank you for your opinion. However, perhaps I should tell you that, although I am a key worker with this client, nevertheless, I am a fully qualified social worker too."

The social worker concerned was embarrassed, but the scenario should not have happened in the first place.

So! Are there good social workers? Yes, as well as some whose insecurity shines through. However, my question is this: Is there not some way of implementing the training material and concepts that could or would alter this mentality?

Anyway, I hope you enjoy the read. And if you see things that you think need to change, join me in making a noise in the places that can affect that change. For all that, the foster care experience is deeply rewarding.

CHAPTER ONE

FOSTER CARE

Who Fosters and Why Write about It?

Having written my introduction highlighting workers within the childcare system, I think we should now briefly glance at why we need such a system at all and why we need more foster carers.

You are either a saint or mad. That is often the first reaction to foster carers. So, who are these strange people who foster?

People have asked me why I want to write about foster care. There are several reasons. First, I want to see more people fostering, as there is such a great need. The number of children coming into foster care is increasing year on year!

Every twelve months, I look at the numbers of those in care and those needing care, and both lists are forever increasing. The big issue is that it seems to be getting worse.

There is a question I have asked many times concerning these upsetting numbers. Keep in mind they are not just figures; they are children in need of care. I use this analogy: Who is drowning the children in the river flow of the system? If onlookers see a child drowning in the river, surely, they should try and pull the child out of his or her predicament. However, if *lots* of children are seen swept along in the river, and onlookers continually see many of them drowning, surely people should ask how the children got into this horrific situation. Is somebody or something upriver pushing them into the water?

Maybe, instead of observing the horror as a set of figures, we should get involved—go upstream and check whoever or whatever it is that is doing the pushing. We should also, particularly, ask why it's all the non-swimmers that are being pushed in.

So, why is it so many children and young people are coming into the care system? I believe, as a society, that we have a duty of care. For that reason, surely, we should be asking: Why are these numbers forever increasing? What can be done to stop that number from expanding? What can be done to increase the number of foster carers? There must be answers to these kinds of questions?

Who is drowning children in the river flow of the system?

Another reason for writing these pages is to expose things that I believe need changing within the system. It is my sincere hope that some of the stories of my own experiences will bounce the right way and knock on the right doors of those who press the buttons of change, encouraging them to wave their sceptre of influence and authority appropriately. It's not that it is all bad, but it certainly could be better.

As I said earlier, I have been to countries where there are no social services, and the situation is very much worse for young people in those places. What we have in the United Kingdom is good. However, as always and in all facets of life and achievement, if one rests on the laurels of "good", doing so could conceivably paralyse the very idea of trying to get "better" and even "best". Remember "good" is always the bitterest enemy of "better".

A third reason for my writing is the hope that my stories will, for some, be fun. Rest assured, I will not be using anybody's real name. As my birth children used to say to me, "Don't tell stories about me!" So, if you read this, and recognise yourself somewhere in the narrative, relax and say nothing because nobody will have a clue it was you. Importantly, keep in mind that your story could possibly be the one that will just help someone else.

A fourth reason for my writing this volume, I suppose, is that, hopefully, some of the things will make you laugh. We are all a bit funny sometimes, and laughing does do us all a bit of good.

CHAPTER TWO

"I COULD NOT BE A FOSTER CARER"

As well as trying to catch the attention of folks who have never fostered before, I am also talking to people who really want to foster but, for all sorts of reasons, think they cannot.

When my wife and I started fostering, we were often approached by others who said, "I would love to do that but ..." Fill in your own blank. I think I have heard every sort of reason. Here are some of the ones I have heard most often:

- "I'm single."
- "I don't earn enough money."
- "I'm a male."
- "I'm a single female."
- "I'm a single male."
- "I'm divorced."
- "I only rent my house."
- And so on and so on, ad infinitum.

The point is that there's a massive need out there. And maybe you are just the one who could help. Allow me to give you some of the statistics from the fostering network. These are not something I have worked out. These are statements from official sources and government offices. I did hear, not so long ago, that a child comes into care around every twenty minutes. Hearing this is deeply moving. So, maybe you need to look again at the, "why I can't do it." Here we go with those statistics.

> There is a massive need out there. And maybe you are just the one who could help.

This is England

- Here, 56,160 children were living with foster families on 31 March 2019.
- That is 72 per cent of the 78,150 children in care looked after away from home.
- There are around 44,450 foster families in England.
- Every year, thousands of new foster families are needed in England.
- For more UK details, see statistics from the Department for Education and Ofsted.

This is Northern Ireland

- Here, 2,592 children were living with foster families on 31 March 2019.
- That is 79 per cent of the 3,281 children in care looked after away from home.
- There are approximately 2,100 foster families in Northern Ireland, and there is always a need for more foster families.

- For more details, see the UK Department of Health website.
- The Fostering Network estimates that fostering services need to recruit a further 200 foster families in the next twelve months.

This is Scotland

- Here, 4,730 children were living with foster families on 31 July 2019.
- That is roughly three-quarters of children in care looked after away from home and family (approximately 6,310).
- There are approximately 3,800 foster families in Scotland.
- Every year, hundreds of new foster families are needed in Scotland.
- For more details, see the Scottish government website and the Care Inspectorate's website.

This is Wales

- Here, 4,870 children were living with foster families on 31 March 2019.
- That is 71 per cent of the 6,845 children in care looked after away from home.
- There are approximately 3,700 foster families in Wales.
- Every year, hundreds of new foster families are needed in Wales.
- For more details, see the Welsh government website.

Current statistics in the foster care world of the UK as of 2019

- In the United Kingdom, 91,441 children are in care away from home on any one day.
- There 54,050 foster families in England.
- Fostering services need to recruit at least a further 6,800 foster families in the next twelve months
- In Northern Ireland, 3,281 children are in care.

- In Scotland, 6,310 children are in care.
- In Wales, 6,845 children are in care.
- In England, 78,150 children are in care.
- There are 390,000 plus children on as CIN (Child in Need register).
- In England in 2018, 73,000 were designated an LAC (looked after child).

Those are the figures for 2019. They are the latest I have. Usually, the numbers go up each year. So, in 2016, there were 63,718 children in the United Kingdom in foster care. That is a number that increased to 68,352 in 2019. That is an increase of 8.3 per cent in three years. Those are 68,352 human beings—not just numbers. As you can see, the fostering network notes that, for each country within the United Kingdom, the shortfall of foster carers for the coming year is, according to its records, around thousands. There are 28,117 children in care homes and not a regular family home.

Maybe you can see and understand why I would write in a way that tries to encourage people to foster.

Maybe you could be one of those 28,117?

A Full Set of Stats

Please note that a full set of stats can be found here:

https://www.gov.uk/government/collections/statistics-looked-after-children

https://www.gov.uk/government/statistics/characteristics-of-children-in-need-2016-to-2017

Most of the statistics will be one year old, as there is always a time lag in compiling them. The only thing I note is that the number of children coming into the LAC (looked after children) system goes up year by year. That could be because of population growth, but I doubt that.

Year on year, there is a shortage of foster carers. That makes me feel very sorry for placing managers and social workers who have a child they know needs to be placed with a foster carer. It also makes the matching of children to carers much harder.

CHAPTER THREE

MY FRIEND WHO COULD NOT BE A FOSTER CARER

When my wife and I became foster carers, we would often have people come to us and say things like, "I would love to do that." Sometimes they would say the opposite. However, I am concentrating on the "want tos" for now.

Jill came to me one day and said just that. "I have always wanted to foster." However, as I was saying previously, there are loads of *buts* and *howevers* and reasons people think they themselves could not foster. By this time, I'd learned enough to know that, usually, the reasons people *could not* foster were imagined and were nowhere near or part of a reason local authorities would use to keep a person from fostering.

So, my answer to Jill was, "Are you serious? Do you really want to become a foster carer?"

"Yes!" was the answer. However, as she went on, it was a case of, "I cannot become a foster carer because I'm a single girl, living alone. I would be unacceptable!"

On this occasion, I decided to take it one step further. So, I said to Jill, "Would you be willing to test if the authorities would accept you as a foster carer?"

A pause and then, "Yes! I would be willing to try."

Together, we contacted the authorities, filled in the relevant forms, and sent them off.

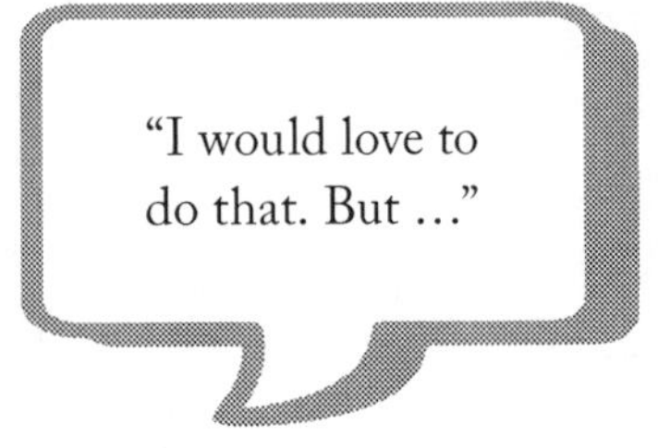

Jill, much to her surprise, was invited to attend the Skills to Foster training course run by the local authority.

After the completion of the form F came the usual statutory process for assessing a potential foster carer. This is quite an in-depth enquiry into a person's life. It includes many visits from an assessing social worker, visits to references, a Data Barring System check, police checks, checks with anywhere else you may have lived, and so on. It is quite a process, but it's necessary if you're going to be keeping young people safe.

Jill came through with flying colours. Eventually, after due consideration, a match was worked out, and a young person needing a home and care was placed with Jill.

So, "Yes! I would like to but can't because," was turned into, "Yes! I can! And look. I am doing it."

Jill fostered successfully for quite a while. She then came to me again and said, "You know what? I would like to adopt the child I'm fostering. However, I doubt I can do that. What do you think?"

With these kinds of things, my approach is to push the door and let's see who or what is behind it and try. I encouraged Jill to push.

With these issues, when you're trying to do something that's slightly away from the norm, everyone gets nervous. It's the "we haven't done that before," syndrome.

However, a few extra pushes in the right direction and the local authority agreed. The adoption was in the best interest of this child. Jill adopted. Don't you think, "It can't be done," should be banned from our language—perhaps?

Anyway, the story doesn't end there. Much later, Jill came back to me again, saying, "Having adopted, and now the adopted child is settled, and all is going as smooth as one can expect" (it was never an easy placement), "I would like to foster as well. What do you think?"

My answer: "I think we should push those doors again and talk to those behind them again. In common sense terms, if you think you can do it, just maybe, you can."

The end of the story, and it is of course a true story (only the name is changed), is that Jill is still a foster carer and an adopter for the same local authority.

CHAPTER FOUR

WHO AND WHY ARE PEOPLE BEING PUSHED INTO THE QUICKSAND?

Over 65,000 children live with almost 55,000 foster families across the United Kingdom every day. This is just shy of 80 per cent of the 83,000 children in care away from home on any one day in the United Kingdom. For this reason, I repeat: Every year, thousands of new foster families are needed.

Government statistics tell us there is a slight drop in children coming into the "looked after" system. Although they also say that figures for 2015 and figures for 2016 are much the same, the government word is that there is little change. I must add, however, that the fostering network reported that there is something like a child coming into the system around every twenty minutes. I think that's pretty scary. The government also reported that, in 2016, there was a large drop in people coming forward to foster. This is also very worrying.

The reason I'm checking all these facts is to see what really is going on. I care and am often guilty of trying to encourage people to foster.

I also want to know if the percentage of children coming into the system is going up, is stable, or is going down. I did think that it was increasing, but then so is our population. And so, what I want to know is this: How does the increase in children coming into the "looked after" system compare percentage-wise with the increase in the UK population?

My reason for thinking about these things—and of course my motive for telling you—is that it seems to me that, if you see people in a developing situation struggling and drowning in the stress, our universal innate sense of human responsibility must surely be to try and pull them out of their situation. In other words, we should want to rescue them.

> Is it possible that there is someone upstream pushing them into the quicksand?

However, if one observes the same horrific scene every day—if, every day, a person can see people suffocating in the quagmire of a broken family life, struggling and calling for help, and every day he or she responds and lifts the sufferers out—wouldn't that person want to know why all these people are in the quicksand in the first place? Is it possible that there is someone unseen pushing them into the swamp? And if that's the case, perhaps it would also be the right thing to do to go to the scene of the crime; see who is doing the pushing; and, if possible, stop them.

Read through the government statistics (and I know I am an anorak on this issue), and you'll see they reveal some of the statistical reasons young people come into the care system. They list as an increasing reason—and these are their words, not mine—"the increase of dysfunctional families". Is this the "scene of the crime"? Is this where our young people are being pushed into the quicksand?

If this is so (in other words, if dysfunctional families are increasing the amount of vulnerable young people coming into the "looked after" system), then should we not, as governments, as society in general, as a culture (not to mention us as individuals), be going to the "point of breakdown" to ask, What is it that we can do to prevent children from coming into the system?

That is *not* to say that foster carers don't do a fantastic job. However, having fostered for many years, I do know that most children would prefer well-organised homes, with "together" birth parents who are bringing them up. I have discovered that birth children love their parents, even if the parents are not good to them. Strange that one, but it's how it is.

CHAPTER FIVE

COURT CONFLICT

There are different ways that children access the looked after system. What I mean is that there are different ways that children enter the system. Allow me to share with you my take on how it works.

1. It could be that social services are aware of a problem. Perhaps the parents of a child, for all sorts of reasons, are just not coping with their offspring. Eventually, they say to the local authority social worker, "We cannot cope. Can you look after my child?" The child then comes into the system and a foster carer will need to be found.
2. It could be that a neighbour reports a problem with a child. The social workers then visit the home and become aware of neglect or maybe physical problems caused, perhaps, by drugs or alcohol. The social worker will then say, "We are taking your child away. Will you agree to this?" If the parent does agree, again, from that moment, a foster carer will need to be found.
3. I have even seen (as, for a time, I was chair of governors of a large local school) a child place him or herself in care. In fact, I have seen that happen a couple of times. On one occasion, I actually witnessed, in the school building, a very young child put themselves in the head's office and threaten

to smash the room up if they were forced to go home with their birth parents. The child was obviously more afraid of their parents than the head. In the end, social services were called in, and the child was taken into care. As with all these kinds of scenarios, a foster carer had to be found. I do know of a very young child, I think around nine years old, who turned up at a local authority office asserting, "My parents are beating me up. Can you please help me?"

> I have even seen young children place themselves into care.

4. It may be that a police officer will be the person who witnesses a child's problem or a problem child and will take the child into care. However, in those situations, usually, the local authority will be quickly involved in the matter, and the police will gladly hand over the problem to a local authority social worker. But the point I'm making here is that the initial action may, at times, have been taken by the police.
5. A child may be in the United Kingdom without parents or guardians of any description. In other words, well behaved or otherwise, they are just here, alone, physically present in the United Kingdom. Usually, youths in this situation will be a non-UK child—in other words, from a war-torn area or someplace similar. And when youths (16 year to 18 years) and/or children (Under 16 years of age) come through a port of entry, the immigration department will recognise a child without an adult and will call a local authority. Thereafter, the social worker will place the child in care. And then, yet again, a foster carer will have to be found.

6. It could be that there is neglect and maybe other reasons, as mentioned in number 2 above. However, the parent will occasionally say, "I forbid you to put my child into care." Then the problems really start. Now, the local authority will have to go to court to get a court order, giving the local authority the power to remove the child into care.

Local authorities do not like number 6 type cases. Who can blame them? They must pick up the cost of the court proceedings. Those costs can be extensive, as well as expensive. Yes, it's a family court. However, there are still the following people to pay for their time and costs:

- The local authority solicitor
- The parent's (or parents') solicitor
- The judge
- The court officials—and there are lots of those
- Often, an ad litem (a legal professional who is appointed to act in a lawsuit on behalf of a child or other person who is not considered capable of representing him or herself)
- The social worker allocated to the child
- The social worker allocated to the foster carer's family

Add up all those costs, and your guess is as good as mine as to the total bill. I have probably even missed some functionaries out.

So, if possible, a local authority will try and persuade parents to agree to voluntarily allow their child to move into care. That route is much cheaper by far. However, it means that the birth parents retain a great deal of control, and that can be difficult for both the local authority and the foster carer.

You will notice that it all ends up with finding a foster carer. Perhaps that could be you?

CHAPTER SIX

WHY I BECAME A FOSTER CARER: "I HOPE THIS IS NOT THE NORMAL ROUTE"

Many years ago, though it seems like yesterday, I was leading a large community of Jesus-following people in the North London area. We had a considerable number of young people in the church too. One day, there came the sort of phone call that one never wants to receive. A young person from the church group, around fourteen years of age, phoned me. She was away with a school party.

She rang to tell me, and I quote, "Please help! My friend at school is being fostered. She is around the same age as me. She is being fostered by a large family. However, the mother and all the birth children have left the family home because the father of the family is sleeping with the foster girl, my friend. She is very afraid. He brings her to school and collects her. He has threatened to kill her if she tells anyone about what he is doing." She went on to say, "If she runs away from him, will you put her up in your house?"

Oh dear! What to do? My wife and I went to see a couple that was already fostering for the local borough. We asked them what they thought we should do.

They responded very quickly and said, "If you take this girl in like this, you could be in trouble for kidnapping. We suggest you phone the borough concerned." In other words, tell somebody in authority the full story.

We did, and to their credit, the young girl was moved within hours. I'm not sure what happened to the man, but I hope it was well dealt with.

The reason why the young lady phoned was that she knew that we had already accommodated a young fourteen-year-old with, of course, permission from the local authority and with the child's parent's consent (more on that story later). So, the youngster from our youth group was not just acting on a whim. She was aware that something could be done.

> I began to learn the immense need and the many thousands of children in the United Kingdom who need a foster home.

So, what next? We (my wife and I) thought and talked it through and through. We didn't know enough about the rules and regulations or the law concerning this sort of thing. We agreed that we should see if someone would train us. We contacted our local authority and asked if there was any kind of course for foster carers. We said we'd like to join in on a training course. We were quickly put on the next course starting date. I must confess that, at this point of time in my story, I had no intention at all of ever becoming a foster carer. I just wanted training—information—I felt I needed to be streetwise about childcare, so I would know what to do if I encountered a similar occasion anytime in the future.

In the course, I began to learn of the immense need and the many thousands of children in the United Kingdom who need a foster home for oh so many reasons, not fitting neatly into any stereotypical or particular box. By the end of the course, I was signing up. My wife and I had both heartily agreed to become foster carers.

I have to say, too, that it took the local authority around two years to finalise our approval as foster carers. Frankly, I have never thought that it was good at all to take so long to approve who can or cannot become foster carers after all the information that's harvested from applicants. I am so glad the government has stepped in and made it mandatory to complete such applications in a much shorter time span. That was a good decision!

I think the social workers assessing us, as well as the local authority who were processing our application, were suspicious about us. Why? We were part of a church community. They were also apprehensive towards us because we had taken note of other people in housing need and allowed them to live in our house. The problem of the system is that we can often get into a fixed mindset that there is only one way of doing things. The boxed-in stereotypical way of the "official system" is one of those areas I wish people would not jail themselves into. Putting foster carer applicants into stereotypical boxes is not a good approach. Foster carers constitute a very broad range of racial, class, and character types.

CHAPTER SEVEN

OUR FIRST FOSTER CHILD

Our first placement was very unusual. Why? Because it took place before we had even gone through any training. However, there was a certain young lady in need of a family home. She was only 14, and her mother needed to leave her. We felt so sad about this, knowing the young lady and already caring about her. We listened to the girl, who would end up staying with a relative of hers who she really didn't know. She had only met this relative a couple of times and really did not like her. So we offered. There was no payment involved, even though the mother did offer to pay for her daughter's keep and school fees. That, however, didn't last. We ended up footing the bill.

Jane was a great person to foster. She was, generally, easy-going. She enjoyed becoming part of the family. We enjoyed having her as a fourth child. Mind you, there were tensions—particularly as my oldest birth child was almost the same age (in other words, around 14 years old). I was perturbed and a little stressed to hear arguments about whose father I was and whose father I wasn't. Most of the time, however, the children got on well together. I think my birth children would, in retrospect, agree that they enjoyed having a "slightly older sister". The fact that she had different colour skin did not seem to make any difference whatsoever. It made no difference, except for when we were on holiday in Sweden. At that time Sweden, as a nation, was clearly uncomfortable with multiculturalism. I think it made it worse with many Swedish people when I introduced her as "my daughter", without explanation.

Jane left us at around 19 years of age to move back in with her mother. I would say she is making a great success of her life. And I am not saying that her achievements are down to us. However, I hope we helped. Last time I saw her, she had lovely children of her own and was married to a loving and supportive husband. She also had a great job, for which she was highly qualified.

> The fact that she had different colour skin did not seem to make any difference whatsoever.

As an adult, she had her revenge on us both by introducing us to people as her mother and father, again, without explanation. Some people did give both her and us funny looks for a while—all good fun. I guess the repeat of her experience in Sweden gave her some pleasurable satisfaction. Then, I had introduced her to people without clarification and she had pulled a face at me; later, in her new country, I had looked at her with the same expression, one that asked, *Are you not going to explain the situation?*

I remember her giving us a look that said, *Now it's my turn for some fun at your expense.*

It was fascinating to be with a foster child many years after her leaving us. There she was—full-grown, mature, self-sufficient, and achieving. And to add to all this, to hear her perspective on growing up in our household sounded absolutely perfect to our ears. I have to say, though, between me, you, and the gatepost, it was not quite as I remembered it all. With her adult paradigm of life and her personal sense of achievement, I think anything bad or negative had been deleted from her memory banks.

In these kinds of situations and circumstances, I am aware that it is a learning experience for both the carer and the child.

Parents do not know it all. We usually are very much learning "on the job". I remember one night when this particular young lady was sixteen years old. She came to me and asked if she could go to a party. I knew the sort of party and the people she would be fraternising with. Frankly, I wanted to say, "You definitely are not going there."

However, I wondered, Was that the right thing to say to a 16-year-old young adult? So, I went away and thought; if you will, specifically, I prayed, asking God what to say.

Then, I remember saying to her, "Listen! You're 16 years old, and you have asked me if you can go to this party. Let me tell you the truth. I am not happy for you to go. I don't want you to go. I don't like the sort of party it is. But, hey, you're 16, and at 16, I think you ought to know what you're doing. For that reason, if you really want to go to this party, I won't stop you. In fact, I will drive you there. What do you think?" Then I waited for her to express her opinion.

She replied, "Thank you! In that case, I'm going!"

As the day wore on, I saw no dressing up and no getting ready. I could hardly contain myself any longer. "Are you not going to be late for the party?" I casually asked.

The response was, "Oh! Didn't I tell you? I changed my mind. I'm not going."

I honestly went out of the room for a deep, long sigh of relief.

Another lesson we learned about Jane was quite a funny one really. It was an amusing habit that she had. Every so often, usually at a weekend, she would work her way through her wardrobe and come downstairs every few minutes from her bedroom in a different set of clothes, asking us all, "How do I look?"

You know the scene, I am sure, and you probably know what our response was: "Great!" "It suits you!" "I like that one!" and so on.

She always looked good anyway. Finally, she would decide what she was going out in for the evening, and as usual, it was always the clothes she'd started the day in.

Every so often, my wife will try on all sorts of clothes and parade, asking, "How does this look?" for such and such an occasion.

My answer now is always the same. "Are you doing a Jane?"

CHAPTER EIGHT

TRAINING

So, it was the early 1990s. My wife and I finally signed up and went on the Skills to Foster Training Course, run by the local authority. The course we went through, and its updated adaptations, still form the beginning of the fostering journey for most fostering agencies and local authorities.

It was an eye-opener. First, the immense need for foster carers struck us hard. For instance, we were told that, at that time, there were sixty thousand plus children in England and Wales in need of fostering, not counting Scotland and Northern Ireland, which probably pushed the numbers up to around ninety thousand children who are looking for a family. Numbers have soared since.

During the course, we learned of the vast variety of reasons that young people come into, the "Looked After System," as it is now called. Some come from situations of violence. Some, just because there is no one else to look after them whilst their mother is, perhaps, in hospital. To put it plainly, no two children share the same need or reason to be fostered. The nature of the needs is truly varied and wide and individual.

I remember some things about the course as it was presented in those days so many years ago. One of them was the way that, because I expressed a faith in God, I felt as though I was being "picked on". To clarify, when asked on various forms from time to time, I state that I am "British, white, Caucasian". One of the funny and inconsistent things that happened was that I noted that, when some of my West Indian friends ("Caribbean, Black") on the course expressed strong Christian views, they were not censored. Yet, if I said the same or something similar, I *was* censured. I asked the training social workers, "How come you don't jump on their opinion, which is overtly Christian, but you jump on me and my opinion?"

Their answer was simple. "That is their culture."

Oh dear! I did laugh; however, I went outside to do so.

I don't want to be too picky, but I do remember one social worker scribbling on the flip chart, and frankly, I did not grasp his point. In other words, I did not understand the thoughts behind what he had written. So, being the outspoken sort of person that I am, I raised my hand and said, "Sorry. I am probably not very bright, but I have not understood what you are saying. Could you explain it a bit more for me please?"

> It struck me in a eureka moment that I knew lots of people who could foster and do it well.

After a long and jumbled explanation (which I still did not understand), I said, "Oh dear! I see you don't understand it either."

Uh, Oh! I immediately discovered that that was very much the wrong thing to say. I was seriously reprimanded for my joking remark and was given a very snappy response concerning those remarks in the classroom. "Of course, I understand it!" I was told.

We moved on with the presentations. I was still left not understanding the issue being delivered.

As I listened to the room full of people working through the training, it struck me in a *eureka* moment that, I knew lots of people who could foster and do it well! Needless to say, at this stage, I kept my thoughts to myself.

One couple in that group had come to learn to be foster carers. And in the process of discussions within the course, we discovered that they had, unfortunately, placed their own children in the care system. They were unable to be accepted as foster carers. People ask me why whenever I recount this experience. I have to confess my ignorance of the rationale behind the action. At the time, I concluded that, if the couple's own birth child could not be parented by them, all other children were also precluded from being placed in their care. That sounded logical to me. However, I have met a foster carer who fostered several children while her own was in care. The story remains a mystery in my annals of life.

In the final days of training, they talked to us about money. Suddenly, I understood that the government was willing to put tax money into the support of foster care. Again, I waited until I was outside the room before I whispered to my wife, "They pay you to do this?"

I have to add to that observation that it is not a huge amount of money by the time you have deducted all the expenses you become responsible for as a foster carer. People who try to do it for money must be mad. Nobody in his or her right mind would work for that hourly rate. "But still," I said to my wife. "They pay you for this, and all this time we have been doing it for free!"

CHAPTER NINE

FIRST PLACEMENT

One of the things that really "does my head in" (as people say) is the lack of the use of common sense. As Winston Churchill is purported to have said, "Common sense does not seem to be that common at all. In fact, I think it may be the rarest thing in the world."

The social services department of the local authority phoned our home after a long while waiting for our first placement. Our two years of assessment had finally been completed. The initial training was finished. Form F was finalised. (The Form F is the legal interview process whereby social workers interview you, your family, and your references and almost write a book about you. I think by the time it is finished they know more about you than you know about yourself.) After the weighty Form F presentation to the approval panel, everything had been completed and approved. Now, here we were, waiting for a placement.

Then came the phone call.

"We have a young boy. We would like to place him with you." Some details about the needs of the child referred to were provided. "We would like to bring him today to meet you."

My further experience of foster care is that all first placements are scary things.

"Can I do this?"

"What will the child be like?"

"Will we cope?"

"Will they cope with us?"

"Maybe we should never have done this!"

"Maybe we are not cut out for foster care!"

And so on and so forth.

As I see it, my experience in talking to other foster carers through the years is that this is the usual subjective thought process for most people to have to plough through. Finally, we gathered up all our courage and said a timid yet hearty, "Yes."

So, now to that common sense that I was referring to earlier—more often than not a totally rare thing. A social worker arrived in a van with a young lad in the passenger seat. There were the big letters of the Local Authority Social Services on the side of the van in an eye-catching font. Oh my! "That is not a sensible way to bring a young person to a placement", I thought out loud. I must admit, however, that I have not seen that happen in recent times. Maybe common sense has prevailed at last.

Anyway, back to this first placement.

We were looking out of the window in expectation. We saw the social worker nattering to the young boy in the van. Then we watched as he came down our path and knocked at our door, leaving the boy sitting in the van. We opened the door with a hearty, "Hello! Welcome!"

The social worker then began to explain something to us. He pleasantly said, "Thank you. But Johnny won't get out of the van. He will not meet you. He does not want to come in or even say hello. I am sorry. I'm going to have to take him away."

So that was it.

Some of my thinking does not blame the young man, transported like a product and a commodity, in an official council van like a FedEx delivery driver delivering a washing machine. There are times when I despair of the lack of common sense and lack of empathy of some people. This was one of those moments.

I have observed other situations and had similar feelings as I did with the above story.

I sat in a meeting once with one of my foster children. The child concerned was at the age (seventeenth birthday) where, administratively, for the sake of the council's paperwork and office differentiation, children move from "the foster care placement team" and are placed under the responsibility of "the leaving care social workers team" of the local authority.

My child had had many social workers. Sometimes, they had changed in very short periods of assignment. I think at one stage there had been three different social workers in a month. So, changing a social worker was no big deal to her. It might be a big deal if a social worker had really connected with a child and been there a long time. In those situations, a change could be quite dramatic.

Why the changes? There were different reasons. Some moved off for promotion, some were due to departmental reorganisation, and some were because of retirement—all of which affected the children being cared for.

I think at one stage there had been three different social workers in a month. So, changing a social worker was no big deal to her.

All this meant that staff in Social Services change departments and social workers—not that the children are always aware or even care. This is much for the benefit of the department, rather than any child.

So, sitting in the meeting, the social worker chair understood the move and change of the social worker. He had done the same training as me, and so he was aware that such changes of personnel could be traumatic. However, he had not used any of the aforementioned CS. The social worker attached to my foster child had only been in placement for a few days. My foster child had met her before this meeting for a maximum of around three minutes or so. The chair announced the changeover and then said, "So how are we going to deal with this very delicate goodbye?"

My foster child piped up and said, "Oh! That's easy. Goodbye."

Knowing the situation, I laughed, and so did my wife.

Boy! Were we in trouble with the chair for not treating things in a more serious manner! It seemed to me he had no access to common sense. He had the foster child's file open before him, he knew how many changes of staff the child had gone through, and he knew how long the newest member of staff had known the child but seemed to be insensitive to the child's nonchalance and cavalier response to the "goodbye". To the child it was a "nonevent". Practical common sense would surely dictate a clear understanding as to why the child did not consider the goodbye, by any means, an important or emotional moment. However, the protocols of the office and the papers on the file seemed to be more important than the child himself.

I know there are rules, and there need to be "best practises". But implementing those criteria should not exclude common sense. Maybe that should be a key part of social work training.

CHAPTER TEN

I HOPE THE SYSTEM IS GETTING BETTER

My wife and I fostered as "emergency" foster carers and also for some "difficult to place" young people. As often happens, we had a phone call.

"Could you take a young 14-year-old who is in need of placement very urgently?"

"Yes. We can," was our reply, and the young lad moved in with nothing but the clothes he stood up in.

As we noted earlier, there are some things that foster carers (never mind birth parents) should never say to children or youth in their care. We shall call the boy Paul. One day he was doing something out of order.

I tut-tutted at him and said, "That is very wrong." I was joking and trying to be funny, but I said, unfortunately, "Do that again and I'll – – – – you."

Very bad joke. I wish I hadn't said it, but the words came out on the spur of the moment. He laughed. I was surprised, if not shocked.

"Hey! How come you laugh at me for saying "I'll – – – – you." I asked. "You've told me that you're in care because you've run away from home for the reason of your father threatening to – – – – you."

He laughed again. "Because," he said, "I know you. You don't mean it. My father does."

I am not recommending that anybody ever use the phrase that I did, but this interaction does show that communication is a lot more than just mere words.

> It did worry me deeply that, for seven weeks or so, I had had a young man in my care that social services had no record of.

Very quickly, we kitted Paul out with uniform for school, where he was doing well academically. We treated him to other clothes too. He was just a nice young man to have around. He was a teenager, yes! But he wasn't a great deal of "work", wasn't high maintenance. He was just nice to have in the home.

Paul had been with us for around seven or eight weeks. We were sitting, early one morning, around the breakfast table eating and chatting together when the phone rang. I answered to hear the voice of the duty social worker at the social work family placement department for the borough we were fostering for. I answered with a cheery, "Hello!"

The social worker started to explain. "Oh! I am so glad I have gotten hold of you. You're on our placement list as a foster carer home that takes emergencies, aren't you? And you also sometimes take difficult to place young people."

"Yes!" I said. "That's us!"

"That's great!" he went on. "So, can I place a child with you today?"

"No," I answered. "You can't. I'm already full and have an emergency placement."

"No, you don't!" was his reply.

I have to say that it always makes me laugh when people are so certain of their position when you know that they're totally wrong. "Yes, I do," I returned.

"No, no!" he said. "I can see from my list that you have no emergency placed with you at the moment."

"Your list is wrong," I gently affirmed. "I do have a young person."

"I don't understand," he said. "The placement list shows you as vacant. You cannot have a placement at the moment."

"Well," I countered, "that is very strange because I am sitting opposite him at the moment, and we are having breakfast together. So, I don't know what to say about your list."

It went very quiet on the other end of the phone. Finally, I heard a distant sigh, followed by a question. "Who placed this young man with you?"

"Well, it was a duty social worker—someone just like you."

Another sigh.

"There is absolutely no record and no paperwork for this placement. Can you give me his name?"

I obliged him with the name, with a rider of a thought. "That's why, I guess, we have had no financial contributions towards Paul's new uniform and clothes."

True to his word, that duty officer arranged for a social worker to call and take all the details concerning Paul. And within a short week or so, my friend Paul was placed with permanent foster carers. But it did worry me deeply that, for seven weeks or so, I had had a young man in my care that social services had no record of.

My suspicion was that, in the stress of a night-duty-officer's pressure, the details of the placement had not been recorded adequately and/or not passed on to the day team for follow-through. So the poor lad had been lost in the system. I guess we had too.

So, let's hope that the system protocols have improved these days.

CHAPTER ELEVEN

THE PROBLEM OF LABELS

Joy was placed with us when she was around 14 years old. We already knew her quite well, as she was fostered for a period of time by another couple in our church community, who had recently found her difficult to handle. Teenagers can be a bit like that. However, my wife and I thought it would be a great pity to see her lose contact with all the friendships that she'd made over the years. As we were part of the same community and group of friends, we held the strong opinion that she would be fine if we fostered her, as she would maintain all her acquaintances and circle of relationships. So, with the agreement of the placing authority, Joy moved in.

Joy had been in the care system from a very young age—in fact, since she was just a toddler. Sadly, her parents did not want to know her. What was sadder was that they lived just around the corner from us. It was a thing that made our new foster daughter afraid of accidentally meeting them.

The authorities, along with the school, had decided that Joy had learning problems. For this reason, she became what is labelled as a "statemented child". This is an "educational term" used by schools and the education authorities to note that a child needs extra educational support. The good thing about that is that the school gets extra money for a child who is "statemented." Added to that, the child gets extra personal tuition. The bad thing about this (in my opinion) is that the child now thinks he or she has a permanent stigmatised label written across his or her forehead. That is a disadvantage for any child in lots of ways.

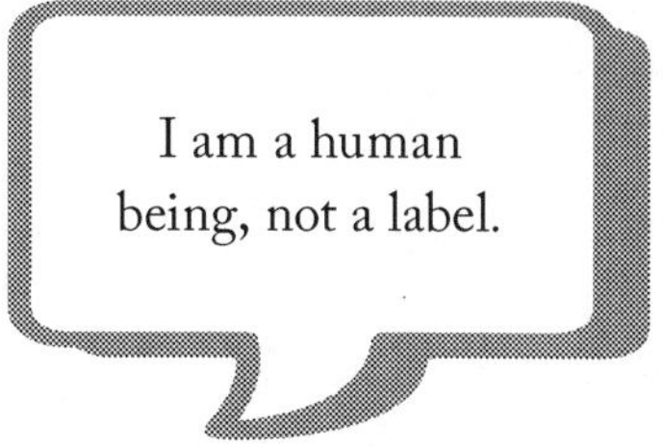

How can that be a disadvantage? you ask. To start with, it separates the child at school from his or her normal classmates and peer group. Children generally do not like to be seen as different or abnormal. The truth is that, if the authorities within society stick any label one can think of on a child—including "being fostered", it gives other children the opportunity to name-call, bully, or exclude. These things don't always happen, but they certainly can and are a danger.

Joy used the label placed on her head in a variety of ways, which, most of the time, really irritated me. It irritated me because, although I could see that in certain educational areas, Joy was slower (that is, she was slower at maths and English), nevertheless, in a lot of areas, she was your typical teenager.

So, we would get interactions like, "Can you wash up tonight, Joy?"

"I am educationally backward," would be the reply.

"Just wash up!" would be my firm and rather a sharp answer.

Only then would she do it, and she would do whatever job we gave her perfectly well. No problem. Label absolutely not applicable.

"Have a bath, Joy."

Joy did not like water and would avoid all washing if she could. I'm not sure why. But her answer in the first instance would always be, "I am backward."

Then proving that she was not backward and actually rather sharp, one would hear the bath running and then lots of splashing around. One can swish and swash one's hands around in a bath and give great impressions of bathing. But then, out she would come from the bathroom, perfectly dry. And so would be all the towels. Amazing.

So, we would start again with, "Being statemented does not apply to bathing, Joy!"

We would supply Joy with money to buy necessary things, with the proviso that, "This is not to be spent on sweets and comics."

The necessary things would not be bought, and lots of sweets and comics would appear.

"Why did you not spend it on what we told you to?" we would crossly inquire.

"Oh dear!" would be standard the answer. "I am educationally backward."

Argh!

Most of the time, Joy was a pleasure to have as a foster child. She was helpful, polite, and great as part of the family. We loved her. However, what to say concerning the label? The downside of the label, from where I sit, is that there are so many difficulties with it. The great aspect of the extra funding and help is marvellous. But how to get around the negative side? Any answers?

CHAPTER TWELVE

BUREAUCRACY WINS OVER REAL CARE

As I told you in the previous chapter, Joy lived as our foster child for a long time. As I remember, it was from the time she was fourteen years old until she was gone twenty that she was under our care. This phenomenon was partly due to the fact of her educational statement, which I previously highlighted. This was another great benefit from the statemented child label. For her stability and settled family life, she was allowed to stay with us longer than would have otherwise been the case. This was before the government brought in the "over 18" rule.

The statemented child label gave Joy some stability, in that she was allowed to stay with us until age 20. But that was the exception; bureaucracy more often wins over real care.

Unusually, Joy had had the same social worker since she was a toddler. That is very unusual these days. It was, however, great for Joy. And her social services officer was a great social worker. She, the social worker that is, was so incensed as to the bad deal that the local authority had given my foster daughter that she organised a court case against the council. It was a case she won. It was a case, fought for her by her trusted social worker, that ultimately gave my foster child many thousands of pounds compensation. I think that was courageous of the social worker to take the council she worked for to court. And don't tell me that whistle-blowers are protected. It was a really sad day for me and my foster child when her long-time social worker finally retired.

Joy, partly because of her slow educational development, was not good with money. So I pleaded with the local authority to allow me the right as a foster parent to guide some of my foster child's spending of this very large amount of money. If such authority was not given me, I believed solidly that it would have all been wasted on sweets, comics, and video cartoon films. She was about to move out of our home into her own flat. And for that reason, I sought the authority to be allowed to give some guidance for her long-term benefit.

The bureaucratic response from the new supervisions social worker was the typical condescending know-it-all approach: I am a qualified social worker, and you are a mere foster carer, and I am going to tell you what you can and cannot do. The fact that you live with a child for seven years, 24/7 counts for nothing, unless you too have a social work degree. Give me strength!

I went on to plead. "If you don't let me help her handle her money, you are setting this young lady up to fail, and in a year's time, she will end up homeless. That will be your fault because you do not really care. You are only interested in your own job and back."

Sorry about that. Rant over.

My plea went unheeded. After all, what did I know? I was not a qualified social worker. I was just a mere human. So, I watched as many thousands of pounds went on videos, comics, sweets, and bad diet.

Joy moved into her own flat, supplied by the housing department of the council. It was in terrible condition. My birth children and my current placed foster children moved into her flat to paint, clean, buy furniture, and repair any broken or malfunctioning utilities. Frankly, their teamwork turned it into a great place to live.

One year later—Joy's flat was only around the corner from our home, and she often popped in to say hi—there in my lounge was a very, very tearful Joy.

"What's the problem, love?" I asked.

She pushed a letter into my hand. The letter was telling Joy that she was to vacate the property, as she had not paid her rent and rates. Talking it through with her, I wanted to know where all her money had gone.

"Why could you not pay it? The money you had when you left us was a lot."

"It's gone!" she wailed.

I also understood that, not only had she not got any money to pay, she had not understood the payment system and had, therefore, got into a total muddle.

I was so angry I went back to social services and told them about Joy's problem, telling them that I had warned them of this scenario—silly foster carer that I was, contradicting their "wise social workers".

They were, to a small degree, sort of sympathetic. However, they said, they could do nothing, "because, as you already know, we only deal with the children until they are 16 years old. After their sixteenth birthday, they are passed to the leaving care team, who have a different set of social workers. They then become responsible for the child." My story about Joy, they said, was very sad "but nothing to do with us now". They told me I would have to talk with the LCT. They were sure they would sort this out. "Sorry, Adrian. It's just how bureaucracy works."

> The system can be so job specific and responsibility particular that the child can fall through the breaks in the net.

So, with a desperate sigh, I went to the relevant department—the leaving care team.

"Oh dear!" they said. "How terrible! However, we are very sorry. As you know, Adrian, once a child reaches 18 years of age and is not any longer in education or training, the child is passed to the housing department. I am sure they will help you. We cannot do anything."

So, feeling more frustrated than I could possibly express on paper, I went to the housing department of the same said council.

"Your 'client,'" I said, "'foster child' is now in accommodation but is about to be made homeless. Please, could you tell me how you can help her not to become homeless?"

I did *not* say she would or could come back home, which is what would have happened if they said they could not help. However, I got a more "in-your-face" response from them. "Who do you think we – – – – – are?" they said. "Social services? Well, we are not. We are the housing department, and if you don't pay your rent, you are out!"

To cut an even longer story short, via many phone calls and negotiations with more senior managers in various local authority departments, I managed to get a new deal from the housing department, which allowed the back payment of unpaid rent to be carried forward and the rent to increase to take account of the nonpayment, as well as a promise from both Joy and the department paying support to make sure payments were secured from then on forward.

Just to make one more point, how we use words and expressions creates expectations that could be both unachievable and/or just plain wrong. All her life, Joy had been told that she was parented by "the department". If you, my reader, did not know, that is the correct phraseology used by official bureaucracy. Know now that, "the department" legally becomes the acting parent. You need to keep that in mind as we jump forward yet another year later.

Again, I have a very tearful Joy in our lounge.

"What is it this time?" I ask. "Have you not paid the rent?"

"No! That's not it. It's up to date."

"Well done, Joy! So what is it?" I felt it compulsory to ask.

"I have been down to social services to see them because I want to get married."

"Well! That's very nice. So, what's your problem? Why the tears?"

"They refuse to pay for my wedding," she cried.

"Did you expect them to?" I asked.

"Well, of course," she said through the snorts and the tears. "They have always told me that they are my parents. And paying for their daughter's wedding is what parents do, isn't it?"

What she thought was totally logical, to a point, I suppose.

Guess who finished up paying for the wedding?

CHAPTER THIRTEEN

WHEN THE COURTS DON'T GET IT

I have spent quite a bit of time in the family courts with my foster children. It's an interesting experience. It does not seem to work as a normal court. From my experience, there is a lot of waiting around. And as I have sat there accompanying my various foster children, I have tried to work out the cost of the cases that I've been involved in. We're talking of cases in which, of course, more often than not, the local authority is having to pick up the bill.

There are the social worker wage costs. There is a social worker representing the foster carer—in other words, me. There is also the social worker representing the child. There is the social worker representing the baby (when there is one) and, of course, an ad litem representing the baby as well as the baby's own social worker. (An ad litem, by the way, is a person appointed to act in a lawsuit on behalf of a child or other person who is not considered capable of representing him or herself.) Then we have the lawyer for the child, the lawyer for the baby, the lawyer for the department, and finally, the opposition lawyer. On top of all that, there's the matter of all the other court officials. The cost of each case being heard is seriously scary.

The way the courts work also is, I shall simply say, different. In my experience, what seems to happen is that the lawyers go around and around from person to person holding intimate chats, finding out what can be done, what will work, and what's acceptable. It's all very nice and friendly. Then the case is called. All concerned sit in a room, where it's obvious that what's being formulated and stated is the formal agreement to all the decisions that have been worked out in the reception area. It does not take very long for agreements to be reached. It's a good system, I think.

Sometimes though, judges are just out of touch with the real world. On one occasion, children were placed with us with special instructions from the department to tell no one where they were staying, particularly the children's family. This was said with the motive that the children genuinely required protection, and nobody must know where the children were staying.

Sometimes, some judges are just out of touch with the real world.

It seemed that the father had been imprisoned for child abuse. He was now free. However, the police had raided the family home of the foster child. This I learned from the toddler, who was telling me in a very incensed manner that the policeman had stolen her Disney videos, and she had no idea why. In conversation with their ad litem and the social workers, I was told that this was the worst case of abuse that they had seen, and the department wanted the children removed for their own safety. Hence, the child was placed with us for emergency protection.

The case dragged on. Finally, after quite a few weeks, the rather distraught social workers, along with the ad litem, came to my home.

"We have come," they said, "to collect the children, and we are returning them to their home."

I was puzzled. "I thought this was an open-and-shut case," I said. "I thought the man had already been imprisoned for abusing children. I thought this was the worst video stuff you have seen."

"All true," they spluttered.

"So, how on earth can you return them to the family home if their father is still there? In fact, although you told us nobody was to see the children from the family, he turned up at the school's sports day. I was not sure what we were supposed to do about that. So, what on earth is going on?"

"Well!" they said very sadly. "It seems that the judge on this case is not in touch with the real world. The father has been down for child abuse, it's true. However, the judge's reasoning was that the previous cases against the man involved abuse of little boys. He has only girls in his family. So the judge thinks they will be safe."

"The problem for us," said the officials, "is that we know that often this kind of person will even trade his own daughters for the boys he wants. We definitely do not want them to go home. However, unfortunately, we lost the case. Our hands are tied. We have to obey the court."

Often, when we move up into the ivory palaces of power and authority, we are often inclined to forget what real life is like. Hence the historical story of Marie Antoinette's inquiry as to why people were rioting.

"Because they have no bread," she was told.

"Then let them eat cake," was her supposed reply.

CHAPTER FOURTEEN

PROTECTION IS ONLY PAPER THIN

Flora came to us as a placement emergency. The issue, constant sexual abuse by a stepfather. She was very young, less than 14 years old. Because of the difficulties at home, she had, sort of "dropped out". Dropped out of school. Dropped out of life. She was a little unkempt in terms of dress, as well as her general demeanour and appearance.

It did not take long, however, to discover that Flora was a great kid underneath it all. She was both creative and funny. And she was a great talker. She was also affectionate and thankful. In fact, as we progressed with her, she was quite an easy placement. It wasn't that there were never any teenager problems or arguments. But Flora was fun to have around and to be around.

Flora settled in quickly and became very much part of the family. Truth to say, we are still very much in touch and have watched her good progress over the years. She still pays us unsolicited visits and even stays overnight from time to time.

One thing that was always hard to deal with was that Flora was a great storyteller. The horrible thing was that we would be rolling with laughter at her storytelling and then suddenly realise this was a horrible story because it was a real story. And these stories were all about terrible things that had actually happened to her. We would immediately stop laughing when we realised the truth, but maybe for Flora, sharing her ordeals was a kind of therapy. It's hard, isn't it, when someone tells you something really nasty but does it in such a funny way that you end up laughing—laughing, that is, until you catch yourself.

Flora was back in school and doing well again. Her dress and demeanour changed as well. She became slightly more confident, even though, if we brought up certain subjects, she could collapse into a heap. I was driving her somewhere one day and, by accident, touched on a subject only to see her disappear under the dashboard, curled up and obviously distressed while I was driving. I made the mistake of having asked her how well she got on with her stepfather.

Generally, though, she was great, and not only with the family. She began to make good friends with her peers, and she was obviously somewhat of a leader and an organiser.

Then along came social services, in the shape of the social workers and placement managers. Very nice they were too. "You have done a great job with this young lady," they said. "Wonderful school reports. She is doing well all around."

I don't have a degree in social work. I am only a foster carer.

"Thank you!" we, of course, said. It was nice to be appreciated.

But then the rider. "Because she is doing so well, we are going to move Flora back to her family home."

This move home, I argued, was madness. "This young lady is now doing well. Why do you want to set her back? Why are you planning for her to fail?"

"No! No!" they cried. "Home is now OK."

"How OK?" I asked.

"Well, we have obtained a court restraining order. The stepfather has been issued with the order, and he is no longer allowed near the family home."

"So, you are putting a police guard on her and her home?" I asked, sort of cynically.

"No, of course not. He has been issued the court papers."

"And you think a piece of paper will stop him going to that house?" I asked with a groan.

"Yes. Of course," was the response. "It has come from the court."

"Oh, dear. Please do not do this," I pleaded.

"We have to," they said. "We need your placement. And of course, Flora is blocking a placement. Trust us. It will be fine."

I am "only a foster carer", and so social workers won again. Home went Flora.

Within a matter of a few weeks, she had been attacked by the same man, put in hospital, dropped out of school, and was very quickly pregnant. The trouble is, I don't have a social work degree. I am only a foster carer, so I don't know about these things, do I?

I do hear that some local authorities are beginning to adopt training in social work that is used in other European countries—training that value the opinions of the child and the foster carer as well as the professional social workers. I think that could be a valuable way forward. Everyone has something to bring to the table and each person's view is considered important.

CHAPTER FIFTEEN

ANOTHER PIECE OF PAPER

One of the things you learn very quickly in fostering is that children who are fostered are:

a. Not happy to be fostered. This means they are not happy to be with you.
b. Not happy to have the fact that they are fostered announced to the world.
c. Not happy to appear any different from any other child in their class at school.

One of my foster children and I had a long discussion one day. I was trying to persuade my 14-year-old that she was being "conned". My reason for the discussion was the amount of money she had spent out of her allowance on the very latest trainers. I was quoting the factory leaving price and explaining that the tiny amount of money that they were priced at as they left the factory, compared with the huge amount of money she had paid for them was a con ("a con" is British street slang for "confidence trick").

My discussion was not going well. She listened well enough. It was obvious that she understood the argument I was presenting. But then it was her turn. "The problem for you," she said, "is that you do not understand the whole picture."

"Oh," says I. "What is it I do not understand about the cost of trainers?"

"Well!" came back the ready reply. "I am fostered!"

"Er … yes, I did understand that part of the equation. If you hadn't noticed, I am your foster carer. Maybe you hadn't noticed me."

She had noticed that, or at least that was what she assured me. But then she went on. "There's more. I'm fostered, and I'm at school. And because I'm fostered, I must look the best in the class—the best clothes and definitely the best trainers. That's why it's very important that I buy the best."

I gave up. My logic had been annihilated. I had, to put it mildly, lost the debate. Probably, though, I had learnt a very important lesson.

"Nothing to do with me, love. That's another department all together."

So why do I tell you this story? Sorry to be horrible about social workers again. Maybe I have just been unfortunate and met too many who think foster carers know nothing and that they know everything. I wanted to show here, in this memory, how important it is that a foster child—*your foster child*—feels good at school and, if you will, feels like a normal person who is one of the crowd.

Now, I don't know if the system has changed through the years, but one of the interesting rites of passage for a young teenager, drawing towards the age of 16 years, is a little plastic card, about the size of a credit card. It comes through the post, and on it is the child's name and—guess what?—his or her national insurance number. This is big. It's huge in fact. They have arrived. They are now classed as a worker! They see this as now being classed as an adult.

Having fostered teenagers and understanding my lessons (like the one learned above, together with many more), I am aware of how very important this piece of plastic is to a young person.

I say this not just because of what it does but, of course, what's discussed in the classroom. "Have you got yours yet?" And, "If not, why not? Oh! Maybe it's because you're fostered" Different again!

I've taken great trouble to try and understand the system, and I'm not sure if it has changed of late. But when I was fostering teenagers, the national insurance card was issued at a certain stage in a child's life and triggered by nothing less than a parent's family allowance date coming to an end for the relevant child. Arriving at that certain age, the system triggers the sending of the plastic. However, foster children do not have family allowance payments made to their birth parents. For that reason, the system does not trigger the plastic card being sent. What was—or is—supposed to happen is that the child's social worker fills in a slip of paper that will be introduced and input into the system at the right time, and *wow*, the foster child receives his or her plastic along with the rest of the class.

Knowing that my foster child was about to reach that stage, I advised her social worker to please make sure the relevant piece of paper was filled out and input into the system. I honestly asked very nicely.

"Nothing to do with me, love. That's another department all together," I was told.

"Yes!" I patiently said. "I know it's another department. But don't you need to interact with that department?" My question couldn't be said with sincerity without sounding accusative.

However, no conscience or feeling of accusation fed the response I was given. "I don't have anything to do with that department. No! It's nothing to do with me."

Oh dear! Once again, it was a matter of foster carers know nothing; social workers know everything.

So no piece of paper was inserted into the aforementioned computer system. That made me the foster carer once again having to deal with a very disappointed child.

I am sorry, but I insist as firmly and as rationally as I can. These small things are very important in principle and hugely vital for foster children. I am so sorry that I am a "know-nothing" foster carer. Maybe if more authorities adopt the pedagogy system used in Finland and other European countries, as mentioned earlier, that will change. I hope so.

CHAPTER SIXTEEN

I AM NOT FOSTERED

Just to emphasise the fact that foster children often do not want to be labelled with that epithet and often will hide it from school friends, I want to tell you the following story.

It's about this particular foster child. She was a really good child, one with whom, now in later life, we are still very much in touch with. She was a genuine orphan. (Maybe later I will tell you that story too.)

This particular foster child excelled at sport. Sport, however, meant she needed a regular visit to the sports club. This meant, of course, that yours truly was assumed to be the taxi driver to the relevant sports club. I have seen a logo on some cars that say, "My children drive me mad, and I drive them everywhere else." Having teenagers in my home over the years, I have full compassion and empathy with that sentiment. There is a stage in a foster carer's life where one finds that one is the official escort for all sorts of events and venues.

From a foster care point of view, this situation brings its pressures. Foster carers end up taking their children to many places, not least to contact meetings, as well as meeting with officials. For a male foster carer as well, there is the fact that he is (and in this story "he is" means "I am") driving a young teenage girl to different places. However, having other foster children at home, it meant that somebody was needed to be home and probably to be preparing meals. So what to do?

Anyway, on this particular day, I was doing my duty and taking my foster child to her particular sports centre. As we drove through the area, my foster child saw a school friend who was also part of the sports centre clique. So I was pleaded with. "Oh! Please, can we pick up my friend and give her a lift to the centre? That's where she's going, I'm sure."

I pulled up the car and shouted through the window. My call brought the young lady running and clambering into the back of my car.

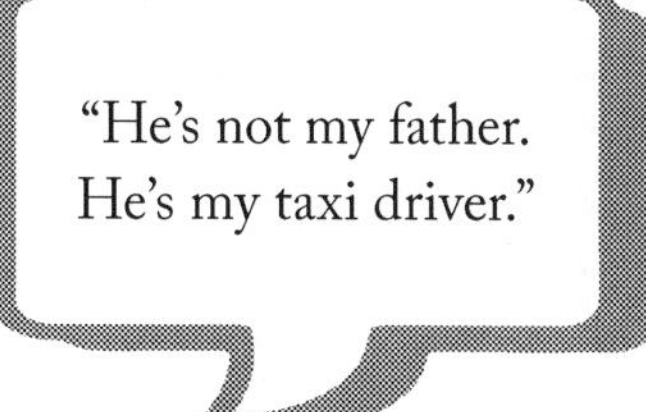

I pulled off from the kerb, and the young lady in the back of the car exclaimed to my foster child, "Oh, Joy! I've never met your father before. Are you going to introduce me?"

Joy, who was sitting in the front seat, turned sideways, enabling her to watch my reactions and gauge the response of her friend in the back seat, as well as to gauge my response at the same time. Then she spoke to her friend in the rear. "This is not my father."

There was a pregnant pause between the two friends at that point.

"It isn't?" said the friend, sounding somewhat taken aback. "Then who is he?"

All the while that this theatre was going on, my foster child was monitoring me, rather than her friend. I just looked straight ahead, keeping my eyes on the road and driving safely. To me, the pause seemed quite lengthy.

Then Joy stated clearly and confidently but with a cautious grin, "He's just the taxi driver." Hitherto all this was said and done with careful monitoring of my response.

Me? I just drove on.

The conversation was at an end. I would not want to put my foster child in an embarrassing position, and so nothing more was said, then or even later.

I have a little phrase that I tell myself. "Always consult your brain before you exercise you mouth." Some would say, "Think before you speak." I think, often, the right way forward is to say nothing. What do you think?

However, I would now like to add that, in later life, the same child (now a mother with her own child) recently asked my wife and me if we would mind coming with her in a particular situation where she had to meet certain employers. She asked us both if we would mind if she introduced us as her parents, adding, "You know my history, and they want to meet my parents." She asked with a slightly embarrassed laugh.

Of course, we were more than happy to do as we were asked.

CHAPTER SEVENTEEN

WHEN YOU ARE A LITTLE STUPID

Felicia was not the easiest placement we have ever had. She came into our care at around 14 years of age, along with a baby—and also a boyfriend.

The courts had issued a restraining order against the boyfriend, considering him dangerous both to mother and child. He was, however, allowed to see both with supervision. So, early on in the arrangement, I arranged to take them out for a meal to see if I could mediate and make the situation better. I believe that they had met in a children's home and started a relationship. The newborn was the end product.

He was a nice boy. But I emphasised that, as the courts had ruled that they could not meet unsupervised, if we were to change that arrangement, we would need to do it through official channels and via social services and the courts. I don't think he was that impressed with my recommendation. I suppose, when you come from a position of constantly wanting to fight against the system, it's hard, if not well-nigh impossible, to hear a rational voice.

The young man in question made occasional appearances at our home and was welcome. However, when it came time for him to go, it was not always the easiest of situations.

Felicia was somewhat of a fussy eater, often complaining about portion sizes and what food she did and did not like. Frankly, she did not eat well.

It was getting close to Christmas, and the fridge was well stocked, as we were drawing near to that time of the year that many of us tend to overeat and overindulge.

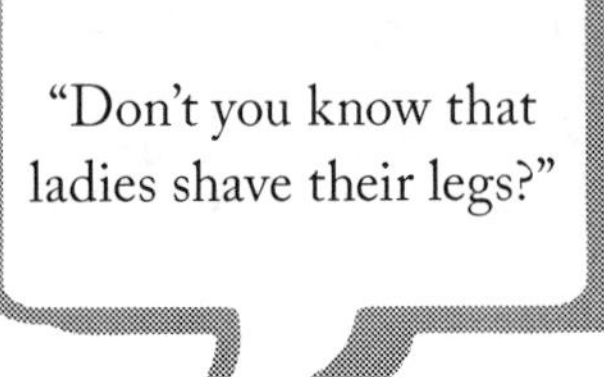

One evening at mealtime Felicia came down from her room, explaining that she really was ravenous. She had sorted the baby. We were happy about that and asked her to take as much as she liked. A very large plate of food was filled. And then she said, "I hope you don't mind, but I'm listening to some music upstairs and would like to eat my dinner in my room."

"That's fine," we all agreed.

Nothing more was heard from her that evening. It was a peaceful evening. We had other children in placement, and the evening went very well.

That evening's occurrence was repeated for the next couple of days. We were, sort of, encouraged that better eating habits had developed with the young lady. Each time, a fairly empty plate was returned to the kitchen.

I suppose I should have been a little more suspicious when Felicia asked me for a razor.

"What on earth do you want that for?" I enquired. "You haven't asked for one of those before."

I was tutted and benignly condescended to with, "Don't you know that ladies shave their legs?"

Passing Felicia's room on the third day, I thought I heard conversation.

Was it the radio? Was it some introduction to the music she was always listening to? I thought I had better just check. Knocking on the door, I was greeted with, "Just a minute! Let me put something on."

A minute's pause.

Then, "OK! Come on in."

I went in, and apart from empty plates, all seemed well.

Only there did seem to be a slight sound, which was sort of odd. And it was coming from the wardrobe.

Opening the door, I found one nervous-looking boyfriend standing to attention inside. No wonder the new eating regime had started! No wonder the shaving needs had cropped up! No wonder! How stupid can one be?

I know that sometime people are afraid of fostering teenagers. I think that teens can be fun. Sure, we've had times when they've pushed the boundaries too far. But often, discussion in a calm, quiet way can bring a solution. This isn't always the case, mind you, but often. The problem can be that adults are not always as logical as they would like to project, are we?

CHAPTER EIGHTEEN

SMASHING INSURANCE

As I have said already, Felicia was not the easiest of placements. We were also fostering other children at the same time as Felicia. One night, during this period of time, I had an appointment somewhere or other. My wife suggested to the foster children that they might like to go out for the evening with her.

"How about a film?" she proposed.

They all, initially, jumped at the idea. However, Felicia changed her mind, as she was wont to do.

"If you are all going out, maybe I will have a quiet night in and just chill with some music."

This really was not an unusual response for her. I wondered at times if she suffered a little from agoraphobia. Anyway, the evening progressed, and we all went out—except Felicia.

Arriving home around 11.30 p.m., I drove up to the house just as my wife and the other foster children arrived. They'd had great fun and were in high spirits. I slotted the key in the door and said, "Welcome home!" And we all trooped in.

Isn't it strange that, when we go into a place, we tend to look ahead and not at the ceiling or the floor? Well I don't anyway. However, on this particular evening, things all seemed a little strange. I could feel under my feet that all was not normal or as it should be. The floor was crunching under my feet, and the crunching seemed more and more pronounced as I walked into our kitchen and dining area. What on earth was it? Switching on the lights, I realised the reason. I was walking along on stacks and piles of broken crockery.

What had been going on? The children, who had gleefully come home happy and full of joy from the cinema, all took one long look at the scene of destruction. And, as one person, they made themselves scarce by going quickly to bed.

Looking around, we realised that all our crockery had been thrown at one of the walls in our kitchen, smashing and scattering all over the floor. Two things came to mind. First, what were we going to use for cups and plates in the immediate future? And second, it dawned on us that we had lost our best and very expensive crockery, which had a sentimental value that we could not replace in any way. It had all been used as missiles against the wall.

> "You should have come upstairs and woken me up, no matter how late it was, and shouted at me in the strongest language for what I had done."

"What are you going to do?" my wife asked, having realised the full depth of the situation, as well as concluding who the only possible culprit was.

"Well!" I said. "I don't know about you, but I'm going to bed."

It was a decision that we both agreed to and acted on.

The next morning at breakfast, making do with napkins and the like, a very angry young lady walked into the kitchen diner shouting at me.

"You are terrible! You came home and saw the mess!" A mess that, by the way, we had by this time cleared up. "You should have come upstairs and woken me up, no matter how late it was, and shouted at me and told me off in the strongest language for what I had done."

I must admit, at this point, I laughed, saying, "Oh! That is what I should have done, is it?"

I don't think we ever really got an answer as to why this action had been performed. My guess is it was a call, *Give me your attention*. It was a kind of, *You have been out with all the other children and had a good time without me. Me! Me!* However, the truth is, I don't really know to this day what it was all about.

The next thing we did was to try and get replacement crockery while we ate off paper plates. What were we to do? We opted to buy more crockery and try to claim the costs from social services. We saved several bags of broken crockery as verification of the breakages. The first reaction from social services, which I have since learnt is almost always the same, was, "Oh dear! You need to claim the costs off your home insurance."

The problem with claiming off one's house insurance is that the insurance premium increases disproportionately the next year. I also know that all local authorities do have insurance that covers this sort of thing. I would prefer their insurance premiums go up, rather than mine.

Eventually, after much nagging, we were able to get a settlement. They paid the £200 for replacement crockery. The only thing was, it took us two years to receive the payment.

CHAPTER NINETEEN

STABILITY

Sitting and chatting one day with Felicia, I asked the obvious question, which the paperwork from social services did not show me.

"Felicia," I asked, "how did you come to be in care?"

By this time, we had a good enough relationship to ask such personal questions. I learned some interesting things.

Felicia, it seems, had been adopted almost from birth. At around 8 years of age, she was told by her adoptive parents that her adoptive mother was under a great deal of stress and needed a break. For that reason, they were taking Felicia somewhere. It appears, from Felicia's account, that she was placed in a children's home. That was the story. At least, that was the story that was firmly in her head. Neither of her adoptive parents ever came back to collect her; nor did they as much as visit her at the children's home.

The former adoptive parents, however, did stay in constant touch. Even when we were fostering Felicia, she had regular contact with the said adoptive parents. They both visited her at our home, and from time to time, she would go to their family home but never to stay, although that was her long crying desire. Talk about rejection!

> I am of the strong opinion that adopters need much more support than they get.

Interestingly, I have looked further at adoption since my experience with Felicia. I am of the strong opinion that adopters need much more support than they get. The adoption service has not progressed much since the '60s, when many young babies came into the system. Nowadays, when babies come up for adoption, the birth parents, often and sadly, have drug or alcohol problems that reflect into the early years of the infant's life. So, because of the background of today's young children's birth parents that I am referring to, following adoption, there's a lot more specialist and skilled parenting work to do. Not that parenting is ever a simple or an easy process in any circumstance.

I think also that adopters need much more ongoing support than they have at the moment. This, of course, will cost money. However, as they say, "It's better to build children than to repair adults." Often, repairing adults is costlier. I am not as clued in as my friend and social worker Al Coates, who has a regular blog on the subject of adoption. If you want to know more, look him up. He tends to know quite a lot about the subject, having adopted six children.

Continuing my conversation with Felicia, I learned that she had, since coming into the looked after system," experienced placement after placement. I think she stayed with us one of the longest periods of them all. And the dear girl was with us only around nine months. How sad. The placement broke down after the wardrobe experience, and although we were more than willing to have the young lady back as part of our family, she refused to stay. Apparently keeping a boy in the wardrobe was more important to her at that point in her life.

The thing is—and I'm not saying anything not known both to foster carers and to social services, as well as the on-the-ground social workers—one of the most important things for a child is stability. Stability is a factor that helps in all areas of development and preparation for adulthood. On occasions, breakdowns of placements are unavoidable. However, there are many occasions that I have witnessed where, to protect themselves—supposedly—both departments and social workers continually move children from placement to placement, increasing those needs for basic necessary stability It should not happen like that. This is an area that really needs improvement.

To end this story, we were shopping one day in a large supermarket, filling up our grocery trolley, when a strange girl came and threw her arms around my wife. After a while, I realised this was Felicia. She thanked my wife for the time she lived with us and told my wife animatedly, “I am so much better now. I have grown up!”

CHAPTER TWENTY

STRANGER THAN FICTION IN TWENTY-FIRST-CENTURY LONDON

I wondered how to title this story. I was thinking of "Truth Is Much Stranger Than Fiction". I have stories, real stories that have happened to me, and occasionally when I tell them, people look at me with that expression that says, *I simply don't believe it*, or they exclaim, "There is no way that could have ever happened!" What can I do? There it is! However, the fact that one doesn't believe me does not make my story any less true.

So, to my story of the birthday date.

It was my wife's birthday. As a special treat, my birth daughters decided to take her out. She liked that idea very much. Off they went for a night of fun in London. They had a good time. On the way home, still a bit giggly and enjoying themselves, they got in the late-night Tube, which, as is often the case in the capital, was packed tight with people. For those of you who know by experience, often the people on the tube in London can be very quiet. "No talking, please! And if you must, make it low level—if you don't mind."

There was one seat vacant for the three of them, but on that vacant seat was a newspaper. Again, nothing unusual in that. If you are a Londoner, you will know our free newspapers are often read two or three times, simply because people leave them on the seat as they step off the Tube.

Sometimes people don't sit down simply because the newspaper is there. One of my daughters, still having fun, said very loudly—not good on the Tube—"I will have to lift up that newspaper if I am to sit on that seat." Her intention stated, she she promptly fulfilled it. Then she began to read the newspaper. Not far into her "news" update, she screamed and closed the newspaper.

"What on earth is the matter?" daughter number two asked.

She was standing in the crushed carriage and not very comfortable. No reply was offered from my aforementioned other daughter. Next, daughter number two took the now-closed daily out of her hand and began to read it, wanting to discover what it was that had caused daughter number one to scream so loudly.

For a few moments, nothing. She was reading thoughtfully and silently—scouring the headlines and waiting to be shocked. Then it happened. She turned a page; read the headline; and *voilà!* again a scream and a closed paper. Daughter number two was left standing as still as is possible on the London Tube, with people looking at her out of the corner of their eyes, attempting to be extra discreet. However, undoubtedly every single one of them wanted desperately to know why two smartly dressed and intelligent-looking women would scream in the early hours on a London late-night train.

> She began to silently read the newspaper update. Then she screamed and closed the paper.

Finally, my wife took the paper and commenced to scour the pages. My wife stopped and raised her eyebrows but did *not* scream.

"This is very terrible!" she agreed with her daughters.

I got to hear the story and read the newspaper myself on the arrival home of all three girls.

The story that had such a strange effect on all three of them was this stranger-than-fiction account.

The newspaper carried a report stating that a man had been arrested in the London area for digging up the graves of demised babies who had recently died and selling the bodies on to witches' covens for … whatever. (I did say that truth is stranger than fiction.) However, the reason for the impact of the story in the paper was because we were fostering the child of the "gravedigger" and his wife, referred to in the paper by name.

Now, I know many of my friends have no truck with a spiritual dimension. Sorry about that. But when one is aware that there is more to the cosmos than just what a person can negotiate with five physical senses, one sometimes comes up against situations where one "feels" (for want of a better word) there is something different here and—to put it mildly—one doesn't like it. If I say that, as a family, we had all often felt—on meeting with the parents of this child—a "creepy feeling" for no obvious or tangible reason, maybe that will help you to understand where we were with them. Anyway, we had, as a family, each sensed something eerie.

So, it turns out that the mother of our then current foster child, who worked for a local doctor as some kind of receptionist, tipped off the husband when there was a baby's funeral due. The husband did the rest.

My son's reactions to the story were also kind of strange. He didn't scream at all but, rather, gave out a long, *Aagh*! "Oh no! He gave me a lift in his car the other day," he exclaimed.

The next morning, I faxed over the newspaper article to the local authority, who took about two minutes max to phone me up asking, "What shall we do? This is terrible! We approved them as adopters!"

Now it was my turn to go *Aagh*!

We did not tell our charge the story of the newspaper, but we did enquire as to what the parents were like in terms of any "spiritual things".

She was very forthcoming. "Oh!" she said. "They have a shrine, especially built in the garden, to contact the spirits with."

In some ways, I was not surprised at all that this child was in foster care.

CHAPTER TWENTY-ONE

MIXED MESSAGES

I was in court again—once again with my foster child. We were there because the boyfriend, who was 17 years plus, had been taken to court for having underage sex with my foster child. Apparently, it all took place in a children's home. She was 14 going on 15, and they both ended up in the same local authority children's home.

My foster child was very unhappy that her boyfriend was being put in the dock for this reason and wanted to do all she could to defend him.

The case dragged on. The boyfriend looked decidedly fed up and under pressure.

Finally, the judge decided on his judgement. He sternly warned the boyfriend that he was not allowed to have underage sex. He told him how wrong he had been at producing a baby with this young girl, who was under the legal age for permitted sexual intercourse. He told the young man that he should be put in prison. However, he thought that, on this occasion, what the young man needed was a suspended sentence. He explained to the young man that he would not be put in prison unless he offended again.

The court finished. I supplied a cup of coffee for the foster child and boyfriend across the road from the courts in a café. The couple talked and then parted. Then we, that is, the foster child and me, headed home. She needed to see to the baby who, at that moment, was being looked after by my wife.

Later that evening, there was a knock on our front door. A smiling social worker stood there with a big box.

> The Court orders, "No!" But the system provides for a yes!

"Hello," I said. "What's this then?"

"Oh! It's for your foster child. I've brought it for her."

I called the said child to the door and left her with the social worker.

The social worker left. The foster child came back in with a very large box.

"Well now," said I, "and what have you got there?"

The foster child opened the box and explained with glee, "The social worker has brought me a great big supply of condoms for me to use with my boyfriend."

As for me, I can understand the dilemma of the social worker, not wanting yet another child that might end up in the looked after system. I can understand the judge, who was warning the boyfriend that if he had underage sex again, he would have a custodial sentence given to him. I suppose I could even understand the foster child being pleased with the gift of the aforementioned large number of condoms from the social worker. But wasn't this a whole mixed bag of varied and confusing messages for a 14-year-old—and, for that matter, a 17-year-old?

I was irritated but without answers. From the point of view of the boy and the girl, this was the same system and official declaration that was simultaneously telling the boy, "You will go to prison if you have sex with this girl. She is underage" and also declaring, by supplying the means to the young lady to have sex with the boy, that the system was not serious about what the highly paid judge had stated.

So, from the point of view of the foster child and her boyfriend, they were hearing opposing messages from the same source—that is, the people in authority who ran the system. I am sorry, but foster children and their young boyfriends and girlfriends, like millions of others of the same age and inclination, do not in any way differentiate between the court and the social services. It's all "government" to them. "I am 'in care', and they are all my 'carers'."

And frankly, if they are not confused, and I think they are, I am.

CHAPTER TWENTY-TWO

ACCUSATIONS

Accusations! I think we've probably been very fortunate, as we haven't had any. When you are doing the basic training, the trainers ask you to put all sorts of record-keeping protocols in place, plus actions and policies to protect yourself from such things as an accusation.

These records often are referred to as "daily logs". In these logs, the foster carer writes down anything that has happened on that day. It can be quite a task when you're cooking, cleaning, taking children to clubs, and generally trying to be a good foster carer to then have to write it all down. However, having a good record of any problems that may have occurred during the day does protect you, especially if a child says, several weeks later, something different to what you had written down—your recording of what really happened.

Although I personally have not had any accusations from children placed with me, I am, nevertheless, very aware of the possibility. For many years, I chaired the Foster Care Association for a local borough.

The thing about accusations is that, first, we are all taught as foster carers to listen to the children. Of course, that is right and correct. However, surely common sense tells us that children are just as capable of telling lies and making things up as are adults.

The second thing that one is taught as a foster carer is that, if you have an accusation made against you, all contact from your social worker and the department ceases immediately and altogether. This means you're on your own. And that's a lonely place to be. When there was an accusation made, the borough I chaired the association for would ask me, as someone who knew nothing about the accusation or the situation, to get alongside the foster carer that had been accused and try to "just be a support". This I did on quite a few occasions. Usually, after an accusation has been registered, any children placed with the accused foster carer are whisked away immediately and placed elsewhere while an enquiry takes place.

Each borough has a child protection officer. Any accusations made are reported to this office. Then a meeting is held, which will include the child's social worker, the accused's social worker, the police, the borough protection officer, sometimes school representatives, and sometimes others if, for example, it is an independent agency for which you foster.

Two cases come to mind. On one occasion, a child accused the foster carer of attacking her with a carving knife. Now, as you can imagine, that is a pretty serious accusation. However, after checking through the child's files, we discovered that this child had moved several times from foster carer to foster carer; for each move, the reason was that the child had been "attacked with a carving knife". Now, one such accusation one can conceivably and possibly understand. But each move?

Common sense tells you that each time this child had gotten bored with the placement or decided the grass might be greener somewhere else, she had used the same argument as grounds to affect the move. It had worked once. So why not try it again? And again? And again? Someone should clearly have checked the child's files before reacting, moving the child, and bringing the previous foster carer's status into disrepute. There clearly needed to be other interventions, in my opinion.

> An irreversible removal suggests guilt, no matter what the final judgement may be.

Ultimately, after several weeks, the foster carer was exonerated and reinstated. However, she had, during those weeks, suffered in mental agony. She went on to foster further, but I have to say that it would not have surprised me if she had said, "I'm resigning. I can't cope with this."

On another occasion, I was asked to sit with a foster carer who had been accused of punching a young lad. It seemed to me, looking at the extremely slightly built foster carer, that it might more likely have been the other way around. The foster carer was devastated, telling me no such thing had happened. Ultimately, the foster carer and his wife were reinstated—the verdict was that there was no case to answer However, there were a few months of absolute trauma for the carer.

I was told of the outcome a couple of weeks before the foster carers were told. There was nothing to answer. I said, "You must, please, tell him immediately, as she is beside herself with worry."

"Oh no! We cannot do that," I was told. "We have to have a formal meeting first."

That meeting took place weeks later. What bureaucratic nonsense!

I have also seen children moved from placements far too quickly and, frankly, bringing damage to the children because of the loss of stability. Surely, there must be a better way of dealing with accusations than what takes place at the moment. Yes, we need to listen. And we must never ignore the accusations. But better social work protocols are needed to prevent damage to both children and foster carers.

In all the cases I saw, I never actually witnessed one case where an accusation was shown to be correct and true. I'm not saying that they never are, but I saw a lot and did not see any substance in the ones that I had to sit in on.

CHAPTER TWENTY-THREE

LOSING IT

In my time, together with the responsibilities I have had, I have conducted many funerals. I knew from experience that, even if I felt very emotional (and often I did), to break down in tears while conducting the funeral service would not be helpful to the family or friends of the deceased. In fact, it would limit my ability to be useful to them in such a stressful time.

The same can be said concerning foster care. Sometimes, when listening to the stories of the children concerned, it became very difficult to not get very emotional. I am not sure that giving into my own emotionality would help the child either. Of course, one needs to demonstrate empathy. However, I am not sure that includes being in a helpless heap while the child soldiers on explaining his or her own particular circumstances in what is, occasionally, a story of pure horror.

I had a phone call from an uncle of my nine-year-old placement. Her mother had died. Hence, the child was in the care of the local authority. The uncle asked if the young lady was with me, and I replied in the affirmative.

> "The mother's sister murdered the child's father. Will you tell her please?"

"Do you want to speak to her?" I asked the uncle.

"Certainly not!" was the reply. "I don't want to share this. I want you to do it."

"Do what?"

"Well!" He paused. "You need to pass on this information. I can't do it."

"OK," I responded. "What is the information?"

"Well … you know that the mother has died. However, last night the mother's sister murdered the child's father." At this point, there was a long and more than pregnant pause. "Will you please tell her?"

How does one do that?

The child herself, of course, had already picked up that it was an uncle on the phone. She wanted to know what the uncle wanted. So, I now had to pass on the horrific piece of information.

I told the young lady, who, not many weeks previously, I had seen crying almost inconsolably at the death of her mother. Now I had to be the bearer of even more terrible news. I, as carefully as I could, passed on what had happened and paused for the emotional outpouring.

There was a deep breath from the young lady, together with a great deal of thought crossing her face. Finally, she looked at me, and then carefully said, "Yesterday I was half an orphan. Today, I am a whole one."

The reaction from the young lady, I am sorry to report, was almost too much for me to handle. I had to quickly make space between the young lady and myself. My emotions could no longer be hidden. I could not cope at all.

There are sometimes deep emotions in the life of a foster child that the foster carer has to help the child cope with. Equally, there are times of deep emotion that the foster carer has to carry because of the attachment to foster children.

Quite often, people ask me what it's like when a child moves on. The answer to that is that it often depends on the age of the child. For older ones, frequently, my experience is that contact remains—not with all of the children but with many of them. So, they cease to be your child in placement or even the child you are caring for. Instead, they become friends or genuine extended family members.

However, with babies in particular, that's another story—especially if you have cared for them from a very young age. When they go, unless the place they are going to is, for example, cooperative adopters who appreciate the baby's history and want you to keep in touch, there are other circumstances that can make it emotionally traumatic.

I am sorry, but there is no other way to say it. It can become quite intensely emotionally draining.

CHAPTER TWENTY-FOUR

BRAGGING RIGHTS

When I first became a foster carer and had slightly older children placed with us, a couple of issues took me by surprise.

The first was how well my foster children knew other children in the looked after system. It was, almost, like a family. I suppose I should not have been surprised, as often there were parties, trips, and outings for foster children in the area. Of course, at those events, they would meet each other.

The second thing I noted—and to note this, you must usually stay quietly in the background and be as incognito as possible—was the "bragging rights" discussions among the children in care. It's interesting to hear children discussing their foster carers. It was all about how good, bad, or indifferent they were.

And then they would discuss their own lives and how they had come to be in foster care. This could be funny to listen to, as it seemed that what one had to do was to tell one's story to the other child or children, and, if possible, make the memoirs as bad as you possibly could.

I have to say that, with bragging rights discussions, my placements usually won, simply because we had "emergency placements"—children with more horrific stories than others. That was why they were emergency foster children. A list of periods of homelessness and sleeping under bridges and death and destruction stories from children in foster care with us would be more horrific than any other child's terrible story. The aim among the children in these discussions always seemed to be to win the prize and be able to claim that, "My story is much worse than yours."

How well the children in care know the system.

The third area that fascinated me was how well many of the children understood the foster care system. They knew very well how placements worked and how one would arrange to move on! They even understood some of the financial arrangements of the programme. And sadly, some of them would, in my opinion, abuse the system. Some, I saw, would take a taxi to get to social services to attend a meeting or to ask for some benefit or other. The taxi would park outside social services, and the instruction to the driver from the child would be, "It's OK! Social services will pay you." And they always did.

Sometimes, I watched children exploit their social workers. Often the social worker would want to make the child "happy". I observed that, occasionally, making the child happy was not for the benefit of the child but, rather, the benefit of the social worker. Their caseload is usually so huge the social worker didn't ever want to be harassed by a discontented placement.

So, I watched, not myself but a friend of mine who was also fostering. His placement, while in a bad mood, smashed their main front window. What sort of discipline does one apply to that situation? I am not talking about wanting to be cruel but to clearly help the person in care to develop self-discipline. In this instance, the foster carer said, "OK! As you know, we were going to buy you that guitar you wanted next week. However, because of your actions, this is not going to happen. You are now going to have to wait an extra month for the guitar."

The child then complained to the social worker, who, for a quiet life, managed to find some funding and finance the guitar—immediately.

In this writer's opinion, that course of action was not in the slightest way helpful to the ongoing stability of the child. It was not helpful to the foster carers, and, in the end, it really was not putting the child's needs at the centre of things. It was not helpful to the child in terms of their future character development.

CHAPTER TWENTY-FIVE

FORGIVENESS

A Methodology?

I really do not understand the many meetings that are held with queues of people (an independent chair, two or sometimes three social workers, the head of the relevant school, the relevant teacher or teachers, the social workers for the foster carers, the social services department manager, and the foster carers. And of course—because, as they always say, "This is for you"—the child, who will, if he or she has one, sit with a hoodie on and head phones plugged into his or her ears staring blankly into space is there too.) It's quite a gathering.

Why does the child stare into space? Quite frankly, it's because he or she doesn't want to be there at all; the child feels intimidated by the entire circus.

I can hold my own in most meetings. I think I am reasonably articulate. And I don't really think I suffer from intimidation in any way. However, if I allowed myself the weakness, I could be very much intimidated by such consultations. Let's find a better way.

Maybe the protocols of the system could demand a meeting beforehand and express all their opinions and appoint just one or two people to meet with the child and foster carer to see where things should go?

But in a similar scenario that I wish to highlight, we were in one such meeting on one occasion. My problem was not the meeting itself but what to actually do. The meeting was at my home. The whole meeting had been called because my foster child placement had made lots of complaints about the social worker. I was pretty sure that this child had done the same thing in the past, and it would not have surprised me even if social workers had been disciplined—or possibly even dismissed because of such accusations.

Sadly, I was almost certain that what was going to be said by the placed child would *not* be the truth. I was the foster carer, and I knew this child.

So, what to do?

The problem is that, in convocations like this, it can very easily get into a he-said-she-said kind of theatre. Then it ends up as a simple, "Fellow colleagues, who do you believe?" And of course, with the regular high-profile mantra of, "We must listen to the child," decisions often lost track of objectivity and truth.

My other issue on this occasion was that the implicated and accused social worker was really a very good, caring, and professional person who was doing a really great job in several very difficult situations. So, I asked myself yet again, What to do?

The meeting droned on. My placement child looked very, very sure that she had the social worker on the run and against the ropes. The social worker was somehow disappearing into one of my comfy chairs and obviously did not know what to say or how best to defend herself. She sank lower and lower, and I thought she was just about to vanish from sight.

Then my wife, "the wise one", interrupted the meeting and asked my placed child if she had a boyfriend. The strange and funny thing here to me, as well as everybody else in the room, was to inwardly be asking, *What on earth does this have to do with anything at all?* One could tell by the faces of everybody present that this was what everybody was thinking about my wife's question. I think it is very funny and always a good tactic on this sort of occasion I am discussing, when everybody's mind is unclear as to what the truth is, to ask questions that nobody really knows the answer to, when you are the only person that does.

My placed child looked surprised. She knew that my wife knew she had a boyfriend. Her glance at my wife and the expression on the child's face gave it away. It was clearly saying, *You know the answer to this question. Why are you asking me this?* Out loud, however, she simply replied, "Yes! I have."

The follow-up question was great. "Does he ever do anything wrong?" my wife enquired.

"Of course!" The child again knew the answer.

As in all families, people tend to say things about their personal lives, and we had heard the complaints from the mouth of the young girl herself. Again, my foster child had responded with an expression that asked, *Why are you asking questions that you know the answers to?* "Yes, he does. Everyone does things wrong from time to time", she responded.

Then my wife delivered the coup de grâce. "Do you forgive him?"

"Yes of course," came the reply. "He's my boyfriend."

And then the final axe to the root of the tree. "So, on this occasion, do you think you could forgive your social worker for anything you think she has done wrong?"

Oh dear! No way out. No checking rights or wrongs. No room for checking who said what or who didn't say what. All she had was a naked, "Can you forgive?"

A deep breath from the child. Brief hesitation revealed a brief inward struggle and then a release of all tension.

> How can this new and exciting "method of forgiveness" be used?

"Yes. I can," she said.

End of the meeting.

To my mind, all parties won.

Or so I thought.

All parties stood up to leave. With a deep sigh of relief, I thought I could now have my lounge and my home back. All the professionals were going back to their offices scattered about the capital. Wonderful!

But no! Now there was a long line of teachers, social workers, chairpersons, managers, and Uncle Tom Cobbly and all queuing up in front of my wife. What on earth was happening? I leaned over to hear what was going on. I was amazed. They were all asking my wife how this new and exciting "method of forgiveness" could be used. Where was it learned from? Who developed the system? Where can we learn it? Where did this methodology originate? Which writer's book explains it?

Oh dear! I left the room and let my wife get on with it.

Surely anyone who's met God or even heard of His great plan knows that it's all based on forgiveness and the restorations of relationship, with both Him as well as people. It's the centre of the universe. I thought everyone knew that. Apparently not.

CHAPTER TWENTY-SIX

GOOD DRAINPIPES

Again, the phone rang.

"Please, will you urgently come to the school re your boy?"

I sighed and agreed to come straight away.

So often—it felt some weeks that it was three days at a time—I sat in a headmaster's office, and I felt as if I was sort of being told off for my foster child's behaviour in school. This was a Roman Catholic School, and whilst I didn't like sitting in this office and feeling responsible for this child's behaviour, nevertheless, I was thankful for the school's continued support of the child, who was, at that moment of time, my foster child. Whilst the school had experienced numerous, quite serious behavioural problems with him and, from time to time, had suspended him for a couple of days, the administration always came back and said, "Yes. We will keep working with your child. And yes, we will keep him in the school and keep trying with him."

Quite frankly, I think there had been several occasions with the child that, if I had been in their shoes, I would have honestly expelled him.

The thing about this child, an early teenager, was that he was bright, clever, personable, and could be incredibly charming. However, alongside this, he seemed to be somewhat emotionally underdeveloped and, like a small child, could fly off the handle. He had a terrible anger problem and would argue and fight with anyone over the smallest and most ridiculous things.

We talked. I told him that I knew about all the problems he had been through. There was a part of me that was not surprised at his anger with life and with the world at large. He had experienced a very rough start to life. He had, as they say, been "dealt a very bad hand". Nothing really had been easy. So, yes! I got it. But I tried to convey to him that, in the world, as he was to grow up, it was doubtful that people were going to be willing to give him any slack for those early times of his life. People were not going to be understanding. I told him that I was sure nobody was going to be as understanding as this school had been. I told him that I did not want him to end up in prison. I wanted him to be great and successful. I honestly believed he could be.

But here I was again, back in the headmaster's office.

This time, I heard the dreaded words. "We are very sorry, but we cannot continue to support this child. We cannot be responsible any longer. We think it's too dangerous for him and for the other students. We are expelling him."

We moved out of the office to my car. I drove around the corner and stopped. We sat and talked.

"What happened?" I asked.

He responded with, "I do one thing wrong, and they expel me. It's ridiculous!"

It was quite strange and outlandish how he could only see this one instance. And with the conviction with which he spoke, I am sure, in his mind, it was indeed just "this one thing". I reminded him of all the other times I had been in the school with him and the problems he had caused. It did not seem to make sense to him. To him, this was just a one-off, and he felt outraged that he was being expelled for a "one-off" prank.

"What did you do?" I finally enquired. The school had not actually told me.

"Oh!" he said. "I got bored with the lesson. So I climbed out of the classroom window and went to the play area."

I was staggered for a moment as I pictured his story. “Eh! But your class was on the fourth floor!” I said in amazement. “How did you get down?”

“Oh!” he said nonchalantly. “Down the drainpipe.”

“What? No wonder they are frightened and concerned about what you may do next,” I said.

“They need not have worried,” he answered. “It’s a very good drainpipe.”

We went home and tried to make plans for where next.

He is an adult now and has a child of his own; a very nice partner; and, still, thankfully, has not gone to prison. He still has those outbursts of anger, however. I just so hope that they will melt and dissipate as he continues life’s journey. So far so good.

CHAPTER TWENTY-SEVEN

FOSTERING TEENAGERS

Whichever borough I have ever dealt with, it seems to me that there is always a shortage of foster carers who are willing to take on teenagers—so they tell me.

When my wife and I stopped fostering, one of my perpetual jokes was that I did not want to bring up any more teenagers. However, it was—and still is—a joke. I like teenagers. Yes, there are things about that age group that can be challenging. Sometimes it's their peer group friends that are the real problem. At other times, it's those traumatic events that brought them into the, looked after system that screws them up and makes it hard for them to make relationships and pushes them into a downward spiral that is destructive.

The big thing about helping teenagers through some of those issues is that quality caring demands highly focussed listening time. Sometimes it does not have to be a long time, just quality time. It might be as little as a one-word response that demonstrates care and understanding of the problems of the moment. It might also require a whole week to open up and examine every worm in the can.

Wearing another hat and being involved in education, sometimes I listen to teachers talking with teenagers. I listen, and I think, *You know what? If you talked down to me in the way you're doing to that young person—if you talked to me in a way that shows me you think I'm unimportant or even that my opinions are worthless, I would also get remarkably irritated. And maybe I would even wilfully respond in the wrong way to you as well.*

That is just one example. And of course I don't think any of us has all the answers to teenagers and their angst. However, again I say, wanting the best for them and finding quality time to respond to them helps.

I say all this in order to introduce one of many stories I could recount.

One of my teenagers announced to me one day that there was this "great party" she was going to. Personally, I did not think it was a "great party" at all. I knew some of the others who were going, and I did not rate their influence or what they might get up to and felt sure that they would not be helpful to my teenage placement. What to do? Should I come on with the foster carer approach: "I am your foster carer. I am responsible for you. You are not going."

No! That would not be a great idea, I thought.

I walked around the house worrying about what to do and/or what to say. The whole party idea seemed to me to precipitate a disaster. I confess I did not just walk around. I prayed. I prayed for wisdom and the right approach.

Finally, I thought, *This is it!*

So in I went.

"Well now! I know you are 15 years old. You are an adult. I think you have every right to make decisions. However, I want to tell you, I don't want you to go to this party. I care about you too much. But you need to know that I'm not going to tell you, 'You cannot go!' That, I think, would be wrong. I must not make or force your decision. So, if you want to go, not only will I support that decision, I will take you there."

This speech was delivered early in the day.

About an hour later, the young lady came back to me with, "I have decided about the party. I am going."

"Fine!" I responded. "Let me know if you want me to drive you there, and I will."

Party time came. And party time went. It got later. And then it got much later. Finally, I couldn't take the tension anymore. The young would-be partygoer was not dressed up to kill but was watching TV. So, I asked her, "Do you want me to take you to this party?"

There was a momentary pause. "Oh! No thanks!" was the reply. "I've changed my mind. I'm not going."

If I had been a character in a comic, I would have a dreamy picture of myself scratching my head with my eyes screwed up and a huge thought bubble over my head encircling nothing but a question mark.

CHAPTER TWENTY-EIGHT

LOVE

It sort of came out of the blue. When it decided to come, I was seriously glad that my wife was there to handle it. I think, if it had been just me, it would have been almost a certain bet that I would have stood there with my mouth open.

We were standing in our kitchen. I think we had just finished a Saturday morning breakfast. We were not doing anything in particular. Our birth kids had disappeared into our cavernous house, and two of our foster girls were standing in the kitchen with us. As I remember it, I think they were passing plates to us to place into the dishwasher. Then, suddenly, out of nowhere, one of the girls said to us both, "Do you love us?"

My wife answered, "Yes I do," without the skip of a heartbeat.

Pretty good so far. However, this was obviously not quite enough for the girl who had asked the question. The next question was the one that would have literally seen my mouth open in shock and left me speechless had I been alone.

There were a few moments of pregnant silence before a quickly gestated thought burst out. "So," continued one of the girls, "do you love us like you love your own birth children?"

Again, without so much as a pause, my wife answered, "No! I don't."

"I knew it!" they both responded in unison. "I just knew it!"

Oh, crumbs! These are not nice fostering moments.

"What is it you 'knew'?" my wife responded.

"We knew you didn't love us as much as you love your own children," blurted the girls, almost in rehearsed synchronisation.

"Now, just a moment," answered my wife emphatically. "Why don't we talk about this in much more detail? I'll tell you what, why don't we take you two out for dinner tonight?"

Teenage girls like that sort of idea. At least these two did.

"OK!" they responded. "We'll come."

So, a dinner date was booked for the evening. I was not really sure I wanted to go, but I agreed to tag along. After all, I as a foster carer too. It wasn't *all* down to my wife.

Evening came, and we all went somewhere nice. The atmosphere was good. We enjoyed the meal, and then my wife picked up on the morning's inquisition.

"Now! About love!" she announced. "You asked, do I love you like I love my birth children?" (By the way, none of our birth children was present at this dinner.)

The girls leaned forward with eyes boggling and jaws well dropped. "Yes," they said anxiously, with mouths wide open like baby chicks waiting to be fed.

"Well now!" began my wife, who repeated the question posed. "You asked, do I love you like I love my birth children? This, though, is not about quantity, which you seem to have made it into. The truth is that it is about the kind of love given. You see, I love my husband. Yet, I do not love my husband in the same way that I love my children. Nor do I love my children in the same way as I love you. Each kind of love is different. And it is different for each person."

How utterly profound, I thought. My mouth was open now.

The big problem with the English language is that we really overuse that word, "love". We love our wives. We love our children. We love our fish and chips. We love tomato sauce as well. Other languages are much cleverer than that. In Greek, for instance, one can have *philio* love. That refers to brotherly love—literally, the love between siblings. That same word is used in terms of strong friendships. One can have *eros*. This is the word for sexually passionate love. *Ludus* means playful love. *Agape* (pronounced /agga-pay/) love is love for everyone. *Pragma* love is referring to a longstanding love. The New Testament part of the Bible was written in Greek. We can read and understand that *agape* love is the love of God for man and the love that God wants man to have towards Him. In Greek, they even have *philautia* love, which is love of self. I am not at all sure what the word is that a Greek person would use for his fish and chips or tomato sauce!

By the way, the girls went home very happy and satisfied with the answer my wife gave.

CHAPTER TWENTY-NINE

IS YOUR OWN ANGST HANGING OUT?

Angst. *noun A feeling of deep anxiety or dread, typically an unfocused one about the human condition or the state of the world in general.*

When one is greatly involved in foster care, one can often see life in a poor light. I know that one sees many, particularly children, suffering in so many ways. It's not their fault. They did not ask to be born. They had no opportunity to choose their birth family or the circumstances that surrounded them. Foster care can certainly give you a jaundiced view of the whole world. It's probably a false view, but it's a view extrapolated from factual occurrences and children's circumstances, nonetheless.

Don't you dare treat my foster child like that.

I know that social workers must face this weight of an issue daily. I also know that teenagers, sometimes, are not the easiest of people on earth to deal with. However, there's a great danger of wanting to put every one of them into the same box. It's also dangerous for social workers to approach a placed child and make assumptions without having read the child's file.

So, social worker A arrived at my house. She was a newly allocated social worker to my placed child. I had not met her before; neither had my wife, and neither had my placed child. So we were all new to each other. We greeted each other at my house front door.

"Who are you?" I asked. "Oh yes! I remember. We were told you were going to visit us. Welcome! Please come in. And I guess you want to meet Joan, our foster child?"

"Yes please," was the answer.

Joan, our placement child, came in. And immediately, the social worker's angst was both visible and audible.

"Now, young lady"—Joan was a teenager—"I am not going to stand any nonsense from you," she insisted in a sharply raised voice. "You are not going to mess me about. I have met your sort before. Well! You're dealing with me now, and I stand no nonsense."

My teenage foster child was visibly taken aback. I also must have looked very puzzled. My wife had a shocked and insulted expression. What on earth was going on?

We all marched into our lounge and took a seat.

The social worker asked a few questions, made a few notes, and then said, "Thanks very much. That's all for now. I will be getting off."

Then there was a moment's pregnant pause. It was a heavily pregnant pause.

"Just before you go," my wife said slowly, "I have some questions. I hope you don't mind, but may I ask you without Joan being here?"

Joan was more than happy to escape, having just had her ears burnt. She was out of the room like a shot. I was wondering what on earth my wife was going to question this angst-ridden social worker about.

My wife only paused long enough to let my foster child get out of earshot and then the bomb dropped. "Don't you ever come to my house again and shout out my foster child like that. What do you know about her? She is a good girl. And I have no idea what you are haranguing her for. What has she done? Have you read her notes?"

A rather chastened and shocked social worker admitted that she had not read the notes, did not know the child, and excused herself by saying that all teenagers are something of a pain and that she always started her first meeting with them like that.

"Well," said my wife, "do not do that in my house and certainly not with any child placed with me. Don't you dare treat my foster child like that, and if you plan to, don't come back."

I am not sure what happened to her, but a new social worker came on the next visit. And we did not see Miss Angst again. I haven't seen her since.

CHAPTER THIRTY

READ YOUR FILES

In this chapter, I'll share yet another one of those not-so-good experiences.

On this particular day, we received a ring on our doorbell. We opened the door to find the social worker for our current placement.

"Hello, and welcome!" we said. "Come on in."

This social worker, a young lady, came in with a, "Thank you!" And as it was late afternoon, our foster child was already home from school.

"I will go and call our young lady for you," I said, presuming that the social worker had come to meet her.

"No! Please don't! Just hang on a moment," she said. "First of all, can you please tell me about this young person?"

"Have you not read the files?" It was my wife chipping in with the query. "I am sure it's all there in the office."

"No! I'm sorry, but I have been very, very busy and have not had time to read it." Rather embarrassed and flustered, the social worker was shuffling papers, turning bright red, and clearly withdrawing.

"Well now!" my wife responded. "This is a very complex situation. And it would take a long, long time to tell you all the background as to why this child is in the care system. Even to give you an outline of it would take considerable time."

One could see the crestfallen look on the social worker's face. "Another question though," said my wife. "How long will you be this young lady's social worker?"

"What do you mean, How long?" answered the social worker.

"What I mean is," explained my wife (*Is this one of those woman's sixth sense moments?* I asked myself), "when do you intend to leave this local authority and move on for another job?"

Again, I could see from the embarrassed body language that something had hit a nail on the head in the circumstances of the social worker. "Well! It's funny you should ask that," responded the young lady. "I am leaving for another position at the end of the month."

My wife then, with a smile, said, "OK! If you don't have time to read the file, and you're leaving anyway at the end of the month, then I don't have time to sit down for a long explanation of this child's situation."

The social worker also smiled with an, "OK! I understand. In that case, I will leave it for today."

And with that, she was gone.

I sympathise with social workers in local authorities that have a stack of caseloads that, I think, is almost impossible to handle.

I also understand, to a certain degree, the need for some to progress up the ladder of promotion. However, we are dealing with people's lives. We are dealing with vulnerable young people.

We should be trying to work for their best future opportunities, shouldn't we? And I wonder if not having the time to read the files is a good way of progressing. Surely one should try to really understand the child who one is the supervising social worker for. Isn't that what social work is all about? Isn't the child at the centre of all that we do?

CHAPTER THIRTY-ONE

GOING ON INSIDE

How much do we really know people? We must ask sometimes, What is really going on? I have been married for a very long time, but still, sometimes—occasionally—I am utterly surprised. Usually, I know what my wife will do, think, say, and even buy! However, every so often, she will do something that I think is completely out of character, and she will surprise me. And then I will say so. In answer to which she will reply, "Well! You don't really know me, do you?" Of course, there are moments when the same can be said in reverse.

I groan when I hear people who are thinking possibly of fostering say things like, "I want a child who will love me."

I know from experience that many foster children do *not* want to be fostered. They do *not* like the idea of foster parenting. Often, they see foster carers as "the enemy". They often want to go back to their birth parents, even if that is totally impossible for all sorts of reasons. So the idea of being appreciated or loved is something that should be put right out of our minds as far as foster caring is concerned. I've seen people who've become foster carers and taken children in and then, even during the sad circumstances the child may be in, exasperatedly stopped because, they said, they weren't being appreciated. Appreciation? Often this simply will not happen.

I do think, however, that we should have expressions of appreciation from our agencies or local authorities—and maybe even our supervising social workers. This is especially needed when we, the carers, are going through those hard times with the child in care. But the children? Well! We can hope and work for it. However, I am sure that human nature is such that, often, appreciation from a child who is simply surviving a difficult circumstance or appreciation from a child who not only lacks adult maturity but has also already endured hardships will simply not be forthcoming.

> The idea of being appreciated is something that should be put right out of our minds.

Having stated my case, I'll add that, one day, we were sitting in a local coffee shop for that "necessary" caffeine shot, when, out of the blue, my wife's phone pinged a message just in. I watched her pick up the phone and read the message. Then she read it again. And then again. Then I watched her as tears filled her eyes.

"What is it?" I enquired.

"Read it," she said, passing me the phone.

I did, and it read as follows: "I don't know how you take a text message and put in on your wall, but you might want to do it with this one. Thank you for everything you have done for me. I love you." It was signed by our foster care placement.

My wife sat there with a great big grin in the midst of her tears. I think she was happy.

Now, the fact that that incident has made such an impact on us and the fact that I am remembering it years later, tells you that it is a *not* the norm. However, it also tells me that one, very often, does not really know what is going on inside another person. I am so surprised when I meet with children that we have fostered years later, and they relate to me experiences that have been good or helpful or something that they have really appreciated.

Some even tell us in their adulthood that they had the best years of their lives with us. I certainly did not know at the time that they felt that way. Possibly—or even probably—they didn't know either. I certainly often wondered if anything useful or good was being put into their lives. I guess the long-term answer is, it was. However, I did not really know what was going on inside. It's nice to hear that it was "the good days" sometimes.

So often it doesn't happen. But then, just sometimes, you may get that gleam of, *Wow! That was a nice bit of appreciation.*

CHAPTER THIRTY-TWO

THE WORST ENEMY OF "BETTER" IS "VERY GOOD"

I have had the privilege of travelling a great deal. I have been to countries where there is no foster care system and, often, very little social work or social services at all. I have to say, on those occasions, I am glad that we have a system in the UK that seeks to look after vulnerable children and tries to protect them, sadly, sometimes even from their own birth parents.

However, as my chapter title this time says, "The worst enemy of *better* is *very good*. So often we look at something that is working and perhaps even working well, and so we satisfy ourselves that we have arrived. We have not.

Whilst our social services system, the regulations, the best mode of operation, and our social work training can be regarded, in my opinion, as very good, that very thought is where the danger starts. I have often said to friends who've gone off to university to get their social work degree or their social work MA, "Please do not swallow everything you're taught. Having good critical skills is not a bad thing. It's not something to be despised. Being able to criticise constructively is a useful function that keeps us on our toes and gives us the ability to ask awkward questions, questions that are seeking to take that which is good and make it even better."

So often we are passive in the receiving of information. Some years ago, I did some counselling training, and one of the lecturer's main remarks still sticks in my mind. He had said it about the course we were on but applied it to all sorts of areas. It was this: "Check everything. Believe nothing." That is not a cynical approach to life. It is, rather, an approach that seeks for an even higher position—a better quality, if you like.

There are many times that I see things being done that I think should not be done or that are being done wrongly. Then, after having made a noise explaining that the regulations need changing, I find that, no! It's not the regulations that are at fault. Rather, it's the person or people who are not following the said regulations and are doing something else, or, worse still, they haven't even read the regulations or understood them, let alone learned them.

That does not mean that the way we have always done it can be assumed to be the best way, even if the regulations tell us to do it that way. Why can we not question them? Why can we not ask questions? Why can't we try it another way? Perhaps a better way could be considered.

Have we entered that kind of society/culture?

I have to confess to being suspicious when people tell me things with great authority and with an air that suggests, *You need to listen to me! I am the source of all knowledge!* Worse still is when they pull rank and say something like, "I am the manager" (or whatever qualification or position fits their great wisdom and authority).

My life experience tells me that, when people take that supposed "high ground", it's prudent to look out! They are probably going to be wrong. It reminds me of an old preacher joke scribbled at the side of the preacher's sermon notes: "Argument weak! Shout here!"

I suppose a lot of the time when I have seen things going wrong, I have often thought or asked even, "What is the common sense action here? How do we apply our knowledge, regulations, and learning or our academic degrees in a real common sense way?"

It may be that common sense is not so common after all.

CHAPTER THIRTY-THREE

CHILD VIOLENCE

A friend of mine, Al Coates, is a social worker. He has been doing some research on the issue of children's acts of violence towards parents, particularly adopted parents. I can see that he is becoming somewhat of an expert on the issue, which I think is bigger than any of us really understand. By the way, anybody can check out Al's blog at http://www.alcoates.co.uk. His blog is called *The Misadventures of an Adoptive Dad*. You might even be able to catch one of his lectures, as he has been around the United Kingdom lecturing on the subject.

Al is not only a social worker; he and his wife have also adopted six children. So I guess he knows more than the theory.

In our own fostering experience, we have not really had to face much in terms of violence towards us. We did have one young man, Francis, who seemed often quite violent towards his siblings and even towards friends.

One of my theories is that we are bound to grow up practising what we've learned on the way up. We learn an awful lot from what goes on at home, from birth and up through childhood. My guess is that, if you've grown up in an abusive home and witnessed violence from men towards women, then your internal assumption might very well be that that is normal life. My observation would go further in that, if a child has also witnessed a general antipathy towards women, be that wives or daughters or just women in general, again, that child is very likely to grow up thinking that that attitude and corresponding actions are normal and correct thinking.

Having said the above, I am, by no means, suggesting that witnessing domestic environmental examples is the only cause of child violence. Anger, frustration, and inability to cope with such emotions come from a multitude of life's scenarios.

Thinking about one of those children who were placed with us, whilst Francis was never violent towards me, on many occasions he would be quite threatening to my wife. He was never actually physically violent, but when a big boy puts his nose on the end of yours almost and threatens you, I think that can be quite scary.

I note also, by observation, that, when these children grow up, they do seem to take violence into their relationships going forwards. What I also perceive is that, if it was the female who had watched violence towards, say, her mother, then whilst it did not make her violent, it did seem to make her very accepting of violence towards her by, say, male partners. It's as if these young women seem to be saying, "Well! That's how people behave, isn't it? It's just normal life. It's what I should expect, isn't it?"

I think that Adopters tend not to report violence towards them from a child for special reasons. What my friend Al is saying particularly applies to birth children and probably to adopters as well. I guess, if adopters are receiving violence from a child, they do not want to indict that child and to credit him with a criminal record from an early age by going to the police. And if they go to social services, the adopter might possibly get the blame and lose the child. I do not know. I'm not sure. We don't hear enough about it, perhaps.

On the other side of the coin, if violence from a child is happening in the home of a foster carer, my guess is that the carer would be in touch with social services and/or the local agency, asking that the child be moved. Again, if it is happening, it's plainly conceivable that we don't quite hear enough about it.

I personally have witnessed conversations with some young people, not originally British, talking about honour killing, which does happen in London. I've also heard them expressing the strong opinion that, if their sister went off the straight and narrow, as defined by their culture or home, then, "Yes! She deserved to be killed."

Surely, as a society, we should be tackling the kind of thinking that sees women as somehow "lesser". Doesn't consensus dictate that this should be addressed by our Western culture, which obviously finds this line of thought as not in line with the British worldview? Maybe, from a governmental perspective, we should be talking about and addressing domestic violence in an even stronger way. Maybe some people need re-education. Maybe we really need to get more serious about gender equality in the warp and woof of British culture and the home, as well as in the workplace.

If these things are not addressed, such wrong-headed violence will continue. We should not be silent about it.

Well done, Al. Keep talking about the problem.

CHAPTER THIRTY-FOUR

IT'S BLACK AND WHITE

Jane moved in as an emergency placement. She was a very articulate teenager. She settled in quite well. She was not always an easy person to have around, as she had a question, or an answer, for everything. There was some stealing of our money while she was with us. However, we seemed to have nipped that in the bud. Generally, nevertheless, Jane was a pleasure to have around and quite good fun.

It turned out that we discovered one of her parents was black and one was white.

The emergency placement turned into quite a few weeks.

"This young lady is going to have to be in placement for a long time. For that reason, we need a permanent placement," social services said.

Eventually, we were visited by two social workers, and we had one of those dreaded meetings where we, all together, sat in a room and discussed the young person in our care, who was sitting there, as though she was an object and not a person.

The social workers explained that Jane was to stay in the looked after system. They asked her how she had settled into this placement, meaning with us. Jane was, from her responses, obviously very happy to be with us.

From those preliminaries, they went on.

"We need to find you a permanent placement, as you are going to be in the system for a while."

Jane asked the obvious question, which seemed like a no-brainer. "So, can I stay here then?"

"Oh no!" was the immediate reply from the social workers. "That's not possible."

"Why not?" Jane asked. "Don't they want me?"

I jumped in before they threw in any further remarks and directed myself to the social workers. "Yes! Of course she can stay with us. We like having Jane."

It was obvious to my eyes that my interjection was not appreciated. Body language tells you quite a bit sometimes. Yes indeed! Sharp angry stares, and sudden stiffness in the social workers' seated posture said it all.

"No! No! This cannot be the permanent place," I was firmly told.

"Why not?" Jane jumped in.

"Well, because we will need to find you a long-term black carer, seeing as you are black."

Jane, as I have said, was intelligent and articulate, and so now she really started. "One of my parents is white. One of my parents is black. This family has a multiplicity of friends of every nationality—black, white, and everything in between. This house always and continually has people coming and going from every ethnic group. The food is as varied as I used to get at home. Why can I not stay with these people?"

"Because," the social workers chorused, "you need to be exposed to black culture. The dominant culture of this country is white. You will lose out if you don't get that."

Jane piped in again, querying, "Are you not supposed to listen to the child? Is there not a right for the child to be heard and the child's wishes to be listened to?"

She was right, of course.

They responded with, "Yes, of course, you must be listened to and heard."

"Well," said Jane, "I want to stay here, and these people are happy for me to do that. Surely that should be that?"

"Well! No!" they responded. "We are going to move you to a black carer."

"But I thought you were supposed to listen to me and consider my wishes," said Jane.

"Yes," the social workers responded. "We have listened. We have taken note. We understand your wishes. However, we have decided that we are moving you to a black family for your best interest."

One week later, Jane was moved.

I understand the dominant culture. I lecture to degree students on the subject of culture. However, I do wonder if sometimes we can be far top doctrinaire and inflexible in our actions.

Possibly, that approach has changed nowadays. I hope so.

CHAPTER THIRTY-FIVE

YOU SHOULD NOT STAY WITH THESE CARERS

"You should not stay with these carers. Even though you like it. Even though it probably is the best for you. Even though they are happy for you to stay. You should not stay with these carers."

So many times in my years as a foster carer, I have seen children moved and often too soon, for what I consider is the wrong reason.

Among these reasons are issues and rationale such as, "You are the wrong colour for these carers." Prevalent too is disconnected logic, such as, "The home should be OK for you to go back to now." Actions are made on the grounds of, "You have made an accusation against these carers. So, we will move you now, even though we have not checked out the truth or veracity of the accusation made. We will play it safe and work the truth out later. However, to protect ourselves" (in other words, social services or "my job within social services"), "we will move you first and do that later." But in all of those instances, I must ask: Is that really in the best interest of the child?

Constantly, the discussions of "regulations" and "best practise" put the child at the centre of all that is done. The child's best interest as the number one concern is, I believe, as a principle, absolutely correct.

Often, however, my observation is that there are other agendas feverishly at work. One such agenda says, "I want to protect my back, so I can be sure that, if anything does go wrong, it can't come back on me." I *know* that is not an easy one. Often, I see social workers in scenarios where they're condemned if they do and condemned if they don't.

I think it would be better to have the "airline system" in place, where, if a member of staff does something wrong, he or she reports him or herself. Then there is no punishment. Rather, from the self-confessed error, methods and procedures are put into place to make sure that that human mistake cannot be made next time around. It makes the airline industry one of the safest.

> The agenda of political correctness can lead to bad decisions.

Often, however, the agenda is "political correctness". I am not against rules and best practises. However, I am against the failure to apply common sense and when, best practices mean, if we were honest, the child's best interest is *not* at the centre.

Sometimes the agenda is one of pressure. If you're a foster carer and there are lots of children coming through that particular local authority, it's not good to have places blocked with a child who could go home, even if that really isn't in the child's best interest. After all, stacking up behind that child is another child who needs that place—namely, your foster home.

Sometimes the agenda could be money. "We have a cheaper way of looking after this child." Sometimes, if the placement was with an independent agency, a local authority might prefer to move the child to an "in-house" foster carer, because it is perceived to be cheaper. However, I'm not sure it always is.

So, yes, sure. it's not always right for a child to stay where he or she i. However, going forward, my plea from my experience as a foster carer would be to ask these questions: Are we really being honest about the agenda? Are we absolutely sure that we have applied real common sense to this issue—whatever that common sense is? And are we sure we have not just acted as Mr, Mrs, or Ms Jobsworth would?

Really, is the child at the centre? And are we acting for the child's best interest in our decision-making? Is that the real honest agenda?

CHAPTER THIRTY-SIX

THE DOMINANT CULTURE

I lecture on the subject of culture, both to employed students who are using my course as a continual professional development course and sometimes to students who are in their final degree year. So, I think I can accurately say that I'm a little more aware of culture than most.

In the United Kingdom, we often talk about the "dominant culture". And if you think about it, in the United Kingdom, white Anglo-Saxon culture is the dominant culture.

Of course, there are so many shades in modern cultures. There is obviously no space to go into that issue here. And anyway, if I did go into it, this piece would be made far too long, creating an odds-on chance that you wouldn't read it.

In foster care, it does seem right to me that, wherever possible, we need to consider the cultural background of the child who is being placed. Wherever possible, to match the culture in which the child's birth family situates itself with the dominant culture of the foster carers should be the aim.

We also need to think through the practicalities of the goals that we seek as a nation in this respect. That goal is to aspire to good racial and cultural integration. Nevertheless, I can understand why parents of other cultures would not want their children exposed to certain aspects of Western culture. There are so many areas, even in our own British education system, that I think are detrimental and negative in their influence on our young people. Some of this negative influence, of course, comes directly from simple peer pressure. Don't you think that we should understand parents wanting to protect their children, let's say, from moral damage, in the same way that they would want to keep them from danger on the roads, stopping physical harm?

Having said all that, we also need that elusive element of human mental resource—common sense. Sometimes there just is not a cultural match for a child in care or in the foster carers available. On occasions, even considering the cultural background, that elusive human mental resource I mentioned a moment ago would plainly suggest that a "noncultural match" would actually be the right one for that child. I know, as a foster carer and a parent with my own birth children, that I have often said to myself, *If something happened to me that meant my children had to go into care, would I be happy for them to be placed with "person A", or "family B", never mind the cultural background or colour of the skin?"*

Sometimes, to be honest, I have thought to myself but not confessed until now, that I would prefer those people who are from in a different culture to look after my children, even though their culture, colour, and nationality is totally different to mine. I often think that they would do the best job. There are good, bad, and all types of people in every culture. So I don't mean this as an absolute blanket statement. It would demand the application of that elusive element again.

What has bothered me, and I guess you might have picked this up from my earlier pages, is when some kind of doctrinal degree-inspired, learnt, and perhaps politically correct decision is made concerning a child's best welfare that actually isn't in the child's best interest. Rather, the decision implemented matches the theory that someone has learnt. Thereafter, someone who is "well degreed" makes it a law. And decision makers then refuse to apply any kind of common sense or flexibility to a situation. Because of this, some children in care potentially become damaged grievously. That is a long and complex idea to parse that, nevertheless, makes a very simple point.

So, a child is moved or possibly placed into the wrong home, even though it could well be a home of a similar culture.

At least the placing officer cannot be accused of doing the wrong thing, as he or she worked exactly according to "the book". So, no blame there. No jobs endangered. The only thing lost in the fog is the child's best interest.

CHAPTER THIRTY-SEVEN

IS THE NAME "JOBSWORTH"?

We were fostering a young teenager who, before he had come into care and with parental permission, had stayed at the home of a school friend, apparently so many times you couldn't count them. To add more context, take note that we'd met the family and the school friend whose home our fostered youth had stayed with, and the friend had been a constant visitor to our home. Get the picture?

So when the young teenager asked to stay overnight with his school friend, I followed the common sense rule of asking, "What would you allow your birth children to do?" I followed proper procedures and rang my social worker to inform him, saying, "This is what my young placement would like to do, and I'm happy for him to do it".

I was, therefore, greatly surprised with the reaction. "But do they have a CRB/DBS police check?"

"What?" I was taken aback. "Well! No! They don't work in the sector. The husband is a builder. Our child has stayed there many times. Why would they have a CRB/DBS police check?"

"Sorry then. He can't go. It's more than my job's worth to risk it."

So, is this decision made really in the best social interests of the child? What really is at stake is a job or, worse still, a promotion? Isn't that the truth?

Some in the United Kingdom use the word *jobsworth* as an in-joke. We say his or her surname is Jobsworth. It applies to those people who don't use initiative or common sense when decision-making and then cover it all with, "Oh I can (or cannot) do that because it's more than my job's worth." Hence, Jobsworth is such a person's characteristic name!

Similar patterns did not happen to me, but I have observed and been informed by other foster carers instances in which carers have been prevented from taking a child to a wedding or to a family birthday party. One asks, "Why?"

And the answer is, "Well! It might pose a risk."

It is not, of course, just social services where this phenomenon can be found; it's prevalent in other social and societal systems that have become very risk averse. There are schools that no longer run school trips as the risk assessment and the paperwork and the possibility of an accident outside of the controlled environment is "more than someone's job is worth". What it really means is that children are being deprived of meaningful educational and life experiences that work towards maturity, simply because it is more than Mr or Mrs Jobsworth—or even another person who has that name either as a first name or as an honorary title—is ready to risk.

I heard from another fostering couple who wanted to take their severely disabled child to another country to meet up with the child's birth relatives. The child had not, up to that point of time, had the opportunity to do so. The relevant authority forbade the meeting, not on the grounds that the country they were going to might be dangerous but because, as they said, "We require 100 per cent school attendance for all of our children in foster care. This meeting will mean missing a few days of school. On these grounds, we cannot permit it." So, on this occasion, ticking boxes was more important to that Mr or Mrs Jobsworth than the educational life experience of the child—even though the school authority was saying they thought the meeting was the best thing that could happen for this child. Perhaps they did not have a box to tick in their paperwork, and the other authority did.

I do often feel sorry for social workers, as often they are damned if they do and damned if they don't. And it's very hard to put yourself down in the right position. I have, however, said many times in these pages, we really do need that CS factor to be applied to life. We really should not just pay lip service to, "The child is at the centre of all we do." Rather, we must put our feet where our mouths are. We must clearly and persistently put the children's life opportunities, chances, and experience as the top priority.

Perhaps we need a cultural change. My motion would be that we should change our name from "Jobsworth" to "I can".

CHAPTER THIRTY-EIGHT

IT'S HARD TO PAY FOR AND PROVE A NEGATIVE

When I first started fostering, the borough I fostered with had a specialist team working with them. The team was comprised of social workers who were dedicated to working on preventing youngsters *at risk* of coming into the care system from doing so. Their aim was to keep those on the cusp of coming into the care system from actually entering the structure.

The way they worked was as follows: When a family was noted as having children at risk of eventually coming into the care system, this team would be dispatched to attend to the family to try and prevent it from happening. They would work with the parent or parents and try to help with financial planning, meal planning, and best discipline formulas for the children and generally be an all-round help to the family. They'd make sure the children were in regular school attendance and assist in any other areas or issues that came up where they thought they could help prevent the child, or children, from coming into care.

Of course, even with all the workers giving due diligence, some of those family suffered such breakdowns that the children still ended up coming into the foster care system. After a couple of years of fostering with the borough, I discovered that the team had been disbanded and the social workers reassigned to other teams.

I managed to meet one of these social workers on a foster care training course. We got talking, and I asked her how it had come about that the team she'd been part of had been closed. Her answer was very telling. She told me that, although the team had worked with many families, they had found it very difficult to give effective proof data that would validate that the children they were working with did not come into the system because of the success of their work. Of course, she explained, some of the children, even with their intense specialist work, still ended up in foster care.

I asked her if she thought her work with the team had prevented any children coming into the looked after system and kept the children with their birth families.

She answered that she believed there were indeed some that were prevented from entering the care system. However, she added at the end of her statement, "How do you prove it? How do you 'tick box' the success or failure? How were we to show that our work was value for money? The problem was that some of them may not have come into care even if the team had not intervened. How on earth were we to prove the negative? It's one of those you-just-feel-it situations. So, I believe it was money well spent."

She thought it was. I think she was right.

On the same issue, a social worker friend of mine was sent to court, to a meeting where a parent was fighting to keep their child. The company that the social worker represented had a foster parent who was willing to take both the teenage parent *and* the child to work with them, thus, hopefully, keeping the family together. The court ruled that the child should go into care but ignored the pleas of the social worker and the would-be foster carer, as well as the parent who was a young girl just about 16 years of age.

I inwardly groaned at the court decision and expressed my opinion to my social worker friend. I said, sadly, "Do you know what I think? I think that this young girl will go and get pregnant again. And in a short time, they will all be back in court with the same personnel all over again."

After nine months, I was proved right. However, I totally agree. It's so hard to "tick box" and prove a negative.

CHAPTER THIRTY-NINE

SHOULD I . . . COULD I FOSTER?

So many times, I have had people looking at what we do—in other words, fostering, who then say to me, "I would love to do that. But I couldn't because …" You can fill in the dots with many variables: "I'm single." "I'm divorced." "I'm a male." "I'm a single female." "I'm too old." "I was fostered." And many others are used. You can fill in the gaps, perhaps, yourself. There are so many reasons that people have told me that they would love to foster but can't. I suspect the best I ever heard was "because I am a social worker". In my humble opinion, social workers who fostered would make even better social workers.

I always wanted to laugh when I talked to people who told me they would love to foster but couldn't because. I usually bring them down to earth by asking them something very basic. "Do you know what the first question is that you will be asked when you are interviewed to enquire if you can foster?"

"No! What is it?" they'd hungrily ask.

"Well, the very first question is—wait for it—do you have a spare room? Yes! That really is the first question you will be asked."

Now, of course, that is not the end of the process. There are lots of questions to negotiate. Many of those questions may sound to some as an interrogation, all in order to become a foster carer. The point is, after all, you are intending to be looking after vulnerable children. So be it a local authority or an independent agency that you're volunteering to foster for, they'll want to check you out—exhaustively. That checking process is very thorough. And be warned, it can be a bit irksome.

You will, if you proceed after the initial interview, have to go to a, Preparing to Foster training course. And that is only the beginning of the training. My experience is that the state of being "in training" never ends. It goes on forever, as long as you are fostering. That shouldn't surprise you really if you believe that you can always learn something new.

After the training, a social worker will come and visit you. I think the regulations say they have to do a minimum of six visits to your house—at least it used to be six. They will write a report. It will look almost like a book about you. I said to the social worker doing my assessment, which is called an F form, "By the time you've finished your evaluation of me, you'll know more about me than I know about myself." And that's the truth.

Following through after that, there are all sorts of statutory checks—DBS (Disclosure Barring System) checks, local authority checks, police checks. I think they even check with the Children's Society to see if they know you.

Some people have told me that they were very afraid of those checks because they had something unpleasant in their past. One person told me he couldn't do it because he had a fine for not paying his Tube fare many years previous. In reality, even, some of our bad life experiences are learning opportunities and can sometimes make us a better foster carer—simply because we have a greater understanding of what some young people are going through because of what we went through.

By the way, you do get to read that Form F after its finished. It's usually quite a long read. When I read mine, there were lots of things about which I said to my assessing social worker, "You have hold of the wrong end of the stick there." They were happy to change it.

Finally, the social worker presents your Form F to a panel of the great and the good—experts, I think. You even get to go along and meet them all and (*agh!*) answer the questions they put to you as to why you might or might not be a good foster carer. I have to say, from my own experience and talking to others, such panels are usually nice to people—launching you out into the deep, as it were, as foster carers. And I don't think the assessing social worker would have gotten you as far as the panel if he or she did not think you would make a good foster carer.

And then, my experience, and I know the experience of many others, is that there's one more thing to alert you to. That day will come, and you'll get a phone call saying, "We have a child here who we think would fit into your family. Would you be willing to foster this child?" Be warned, that day-one experience can be a little scary.

But get over it, and you'll find that there are probably many positives to making a difference in a young person's life. I have found that to be true.

CHAPTER FORTY

THE POSITIVES AND NEGATIVES OF FOSTERING

There are positives and negatives to fostering, just like there are for anything else.

Let's start with the negatives so that I can end on a positive note. I would say several of the negatives I have experienced so far include the following:

1. Having things that you own smashed up
2. Occasionally having money stolen
3. Of course, having to deal sometimes with a child or teenager being stroppy

There was a funny thing in our house. We had a lounge with no TV in it. We are fortunate in that we have another lounge where there *is* a TV. Very often, our foster children would refer to the TV lounge as "the noisy room" and the lounge without the TV as "the talking room". If there was conflict, this was often the place where we would sit down to try and sort things out. It was the room where negatives were made positives.

Now for the positive side of things:

1. Well, for me, the first surprise, once I commenced fostering, was that I was given money for doing it. I must have been very naive. When I first did the training, I thought that fostering was a voluntary opportunity that would cost me. I am sure my readers are not that daft. However, I would still say that, if anyone starts fostering for the money, he or she must be somewhat crazy—especially if you calculate the hourly rate. If you are thinking of helping by becoming a foster carer, please do not do it for the money. That would be a very ill-thought-out and bad reason!
2. One of our children, on a particular occasion, sent my wife (I've mentioned this before) a text message saying, "I don't know how you get this off the phone. You may want to put it on the wall, because I know I have never said it before and I probably won't ever again, but I wanted to text you to say, I love you." Now that is a very wonderful reward. And I don't know about you, but I'd put that down as a positive.

A friend of mine, who also fosters, recently told me that a foster child, who had now left his home, as she was grown up, had just sent him a Father's Day card. It read, "Happy Father's Day. You will never know how much you have helped me in the hard times. For the first time in my life, I have felt secure and loved, and you have taught me what it means to have unconditional love for someone." Wow! Emotional or what? Positive or what?

There are even those occasions when you really did not know if you had succeeded in passing on anything positive to someone. You hoped you had, but had you? Recently, we were in the other side of the city at a friend's birthday party. I looked around to see a young lady with her arms wrapped around my wife. Moving over from my current conversation at the party in order to see who this new "blanket person" was, I realised it was one of our foster children from many years past—now grown up, married, and with her own children. It was great to see her.

After the party, on the way home, I asked my wife, "What did June say to you?"

My wife, somewhat emotional, said, "She thanked us for the best period of her growing up life. She said that she wished that social services had not taken her away from our home."

So, there is a brief take of mine on some of the negatives and positives of fostering.

And I have to say, when you get to hear them, the positives are incredibly gratifying.

CHAPTER FORTY-ONE

STABILITY

Social services, foster carers, and the government all know that one of the best things you can give to children, especially those in the looked after system is stability.

I noted very early on in my fostering experience the difference between my birth children and my foster children in terms of stability. If I had to go away, and for work I often did, my birth children would ask where I was going. Then they would say, "Have a great time," and, "Don't forget to bring us back a present."

On the other side, the foster children of a similar age would be much more nervous. "Where are you going?" "When are you coming back?" "How long will you be away?" "Who will look after me while you are gone?" "What if something happens to you while you're away?" And I'd be asked lots more what ifs.

My birth children were secure. *Their thoughts were, He's going away. That's fine. He'll come back. And maybe we'll get some goodies.* My foster children were generally much more nervous. Stability was being rocked.

Wherever possible, whenever a child is moved into care or moved from one foster carer to another, the social workers will try very hard to make sure that the same school is maintained, unless there are very special circumstances with the school. Why? Because they, and we, all know that, quite often, school is or has been, in a volatile child's upbringing, the area of greatest stability. And stability is very good for us all.

> When children have many moves, it's difficult for them to form sustainable long-term relationships.

I always marvel that, knowing this, we don't all work harder to make more areas of stability. I witness children being moved from one carer to another. Sometimes, they are moved very quickly. Maybe the child has had a fallout and made an accusation against the foster carer. Yes! Sometimes the right thing to do is to, indeed, move the child quickly. However, I wonder if, many times, the right thing might be to maintain that stability and look very carefully at what the accusation is. Is it true? Is it a reaction, possibly, to some necessary discipline? Or is it a contrived "for this, we-move-the-child-out" reason?

We also know that, when children have many moves, it's really difficult for them to form sustainable long-term relationships. We damage their attachment processes. And that makes for very detrimental life chances, not just in the immediate term but also in their long-term future on into adulthood. Sometimes we end up giving a child what he or she wants but what will ultimately be very bad for him or her. I think we should take that into consideration when we're moving children around.

I had one young lady in our care at around the age of 14. She stayed with us for around nine months. From our point of view, we were happy for the placement to continue, and really, it should have done so. Talking to the young lady, we learned she'd lost count of how many foster homes she'd lived in.

That really was not good for her. I have to say, she wasn't the easiest placement. However, it was not so bad that she could not have stayed. Yet, because of a disagreement on one of her actions, she insisted on being moved, and social services complied. Getting what you want, at certain ages, is not what you really need.

CHAPTER FORTY-TWO

SPIRITUALITY

When we first started fostering, I was slightly amused when social workers placed children with us. They would say of us, in our presence, "These people go to church. They are Christians. But you do not need to take note of any of that or be influenced by any of it." It was really sort of strange.

I think what was not understood is that following Jesus is not a religion but, rather, a relationship. As part of that relationship, if we follow His example of teaching, we note plainly that it is of a very different quality to our country's current style of living. What I mean by that is that our British current style of living is rather from mouth to ear, my brain to yours. Jesus, on the other hand, took twelve people and lived with them for three years—all of them eating, drinking, and travelling together. I'm not sure about the holidays.

We need to understand that life influences life. So, when we spend a lot of time with people, especially if we like those people, especially if eventually see them as friends, it does not matter if people say, "Take no notice," or, "Don't be influenced." We cannot help but be affected. And often we will want to be influenced, particularly if the lifestyle having influence on us is one that we like—a lifestyle and a worldview that impresses us and one that we will want to emulate.

Embarrassingly for me, without any discussion or solicitation from us, often my foster children would say to officials, "I want to have and enjoy a family lifestyle like my foster carers do."

> Following Jesus is not a religion but, rather, a relationship.

I noted as the years went by that even the social workers' attitudes changed. I could only conclude that, somehow, they'd decided I was not as weird as they had first suspected. Anyway, their attitude towards us changed, and often they would say to children being placed, "These people go to a kind of church. You don't have to. But maybe you would like to go with them." Funny? Or what?

I have said earlier that I was surprised to meet one of my foster children in later life and hear feedback from her own lips about my own values and way of living. I'd thought this had no bearing on that child's life. And yet now she was plainly being the person she wanted to be and was a follower of Jesus. She saw those values as good values to live by. I must confess to having been very delighted, even though I was most surprised.

On yet another occasion, which I think we need to think about, a senior manager, speaking to my wife about the placement of children, said, "You know what? I am not religious." Funny how people always use that word.

I always say that I am not religious. And it seems to me that Jesus had most of His problems not with the legal system but with the religious people and their systems. He constantly conflicted with them.

Anyway, this manager went on to say, "Although I am not religious, I think that officialdom—social services—have ignored all spirituality to the detriment of the children that are in the looked after system. You see, we care about the safety, health, social experience, education, and self-awareness of the children, but we completely ignore (even deny that it exists) any kind of spiritual dimension to their personhood. And," he added, "I think we are missing out. I am not religious. I don't care what kind of spirituality the children are exposed to. But I don't think we should ignore spirituality as though that part of a person did not exist."

Well, I am totally in agreement with him—although I'm not sure it doesn't matter which kind of spirituality children are exposed to. I can think of a lot I would not want children to be influenced by that is "spiritual". But that's another subject altogether.

CHAPTER FORTY-THREE

LEAVING

I think that one of the hardest issues and facts of life in fostering is the leaving time. I should imagine it's worse for mothers when they have been fostering a baby, sometimes for two years, and then the baby becomes due for adoption. Even though the foster carer knew what the end game was—that this was where it was always going with this child—when the time arrives, all those emotional attachments that had been made, some you did not know you had, come tumbling out. It can be agonising.

I have sat with fostering friends who have been in emotional pieces for quite a few weeks after a baby has gone. When you talk to them, which you should do, there is a logic there. "I knew this was coming. It's the right thing to do. It's the right thing for this child." The problem with logic is that it does not dissipate the emotional pain.

We fostered a young lady who was 14 years old and had a new-born baby. Yes, we got attached to the young lady, but we sure did get attached to that baby. Because the young mother was very inexperienced and still very much a child herself, a lot of care and nursing ended up being done by my wife and myself. Unless one is a robot, a person cannot help but get emotionally attached.

Most agencies are aware of the emotional trauma at the point of leaving, or should I say loss, and they try very hard to be helpful and talk the right talk. In the end, however, I don't think there's any way of preventing the pain.

I would imagine that there are those people who say things like, "I never let myself get attached to people because they let you down, and I can't take the hurt." The problem with that approach to life is that you become a lonely island. Human relationships always involve the risk of loss and pain. In the end, as they say, there are only two certainties in life—death and taxes. So, unless you're going to live as an island, you can only accept the pleasures of caring, the joy of relationships, and the benefit of community. These joys of human existence will ultimately end. That's life.

In some fostering situations, perhaps where there has been an adoption taking place and the adopting parents are not the kind of people who feel threatened by previous foster carers, I have witnessed the adoptive parents sometimes keep the original foster carers updated with photos and reports of their child's development. I have seen that practise greatly relieve a lot of the pain in the hearts of foster carers who fostered and loved the child prior to adoption. Unfortunately, however, some adoptive parents do feel threatened by previous foster carers and seek to immediately cut all ties with any adults that had previous responsibility for the child that is now theirs.

Our personal exhilarating experience is that we often get to meet the baby we have years previously fostered, now possibly a late teenager or even in their twenties. They are always puzzled that this "strange couple" seem to know their name and their history and even go so far as to ask them about family, friends, and relationships. In this situation, the young adult who was previously, for a time, "our baby" responds very quizzically. We see written all over their faces an expression that is asking the obvious: *How on earth does this stranger know all this about me and my life?*

Actually, of course, we are not strangers at all. For many months she was, sort of, "our child".

CHAPTER FORTY-FOUR

A SOCIAL WORKER'S ENCOURAGEMENT

One of the frustrations of fostering is that one often feels, at least I do, that what one has contributed to some child's life, especially a teenager, is insufficient. What I mean by that is that, often, children in the care system have had traumatic life experiences that have brought them to you. This is not the case for all children in the system, of course, but it's true for many of them. And what one wants to do, at least I do, is to put into their lives something that will help them in the future, something that will enable them to be all that they could be and will assist them in leading a life that is fulfilled. I have often, however, felt that I had not succeeded in that respect.

Often, the problem is that you do not have the child with you long enough. Children in your temporary care may be just at the edge of leaving the system. Or circumstances may take them back to their birth homes. Or perhaps a breakdown occurs, and they no longer stay with you.

One day, a social worker said to a group of us, "What you must realise is that, even though you may have a child placed with you for just a very short time, your priority is to make that time as beneficial and as useful to the child as possible. You probably will end up putting in something good, even if it's only a small piece of life's puzzle that will be with them forever."

She was correct. I have had the privilege of seeing young people who lived with me much later in their journey of life, and I have been amazed at some of the things that they've told me. "Living with you was the best thing that happened to me," was one of the best sentences I ever heard from a former foster child. I hope they are not just being nice. One mature young lady told someone in my presence about the "great values for life" I'd instilled. I thought to myself, *Goodness gracious! I thought none of that had gone in.*

Another young person who left us, partly because of a breakdown of the placement he created, said, "I really should never have left your home. It did the best things for me." We are now very good long-term friends.

I need to state clearly that we do *not* hear that from all of those who went through our home. There are many we do not see again, as they have progressed on in life. Some of the very little ones probably don't even remember being in our care. However, taking that social worker's advice and having the privilege of just a few instances of feedback from the placements we have met later on in life's journey, I have to say that we are encouraged. We feel, somehow, that much of it was worthwhile. I am saying that, even though it doesn't happen as much as we would like it to, it feels like learning that you have made a difference in a child's life is one of the greatest rewards of fostering.

Of course, I must say—I have to say—that if you, in your own life, don't have good values and an understanding of how to navigate life's jungle and you don't possess something within, a part of yourself that is worth passing on, then you probably will not be able to help.

But certainly, that social worker was right. Sometimes, even small, good contributions to a young person's life will be of good benefit up and along life's road.

CHAPTER FORTY-FIVE

ON THE PROBLEM OF BEING GRATEFUL

One of the most difficult things, I think, to communicate to foster carers is the fact that children coming into the LAC (looked after children) system are not wanting to be in that classification.

I have come across a couple of cases where this abhorrence of the stigma of being in care was overshadowed by the child's own cry for help. One child who attended a school where I was a governor threatened the head with dire consequences if she did not refer him to social services and have him taken into care. She did, and he was. Another child, I think he was nine years old at the time, tramped the streets asking where the social services office was and finally turned up at the local authority offices, asking them, "Please take me into care. I am so afraid of my parents."

Those, however, are extremely unusual situations. Many children do not understand that they may be in serious danger among those who really should be protecting and nurturing them. Many who come into the LAC system have grown up with violence, possibly drunkenness, and perhaps even drug abuse. To them, this is "normal life". And if it's not *your* normal kind of life, you are not going to immediately understand where they are coming from. They certainly will not understand what most of my readers would likely consider as normal.

So when I hear foster carers say things like, "I want the child to love me," I want to groan. Maybe a child will love the carer, but often he or she won't. Rather LAC children may see you even as the enemy or the terrible person who is in cahoots with a government department that has separated them from their mother, father, or both. It's not always easy to get the children to understand that you're there for their safety. You're there for their nurturing and for their best interests. Many times, you may have a parental love and a motive to care for them, which will not be seen or understood by them.

I recently watched a situation where dispirited foster carers, who had only tried to do the right thing—the best thing, the good thing—had what they'd done thrown back in their face. They later came to me to explain how they could not understand why these children were not grateful. "Why are they not thanking us? Why? Why?"

When I hear foster carers say things like, "I want the child to love me," I want to groan.

The harsh reality of life is that, often, foster children (like all children) are not thankful. And, even worse, just as often, they do not even understand why you think they should be giving you thanks. Particularly, in the early days of a placement, we have often been faced with a child explaining why he or she can just go home to his or her parents—usually referring to his or her mother. The fact that the same mother has put them in grave danger or maybe has even beaten them does not seem to compute. Maybe it's that blood tie that blinds them to some things. I don't really know. However, what I do know is that, if you're looking for thanks, grateful appreciation, or love even, you are probably going to be very often disappointed.

Up the road, maybe many years hence, there will be those who, having rationally analysed their own upbringing, think back and retrospectively say, "Those were great people who looked after me. I did not know it at the time, but they really cared for me." Sometimes, amazingly, they may even knock on your door and say, "I have come to say thank you for what you did for me." But don't hold your breath.

There is a great video on YouTube. I hope it's still there. Find it and have a look. I would recommend that all foster carers view it. Yes, it is American (I think), but it's also universally true. Have a thoughtful glance at it if you can. It is called *The Power of One Caring Adult*, and it can be found at https://www.youtube.com/watch?v=u_Oapo1Q7_w.

So, what should we do? We should care, love, nurture, and plan for each child's best good anyway, no matter what.

CHAPTER FORTY-SIX

UNCONDITIONAL LOVE

The problem with the word "love" in the English language is that the word has so many uses. (I mentioned this point in a previous chapter, but it's worth repeating.) You love your children, your foster children, and your husband or wife. You may even utilise the word love to express how you feel about tomato ketchup, sport, and so on. Greek in particular, has different words for the various definitions of what, in English, is simply the single word "love". So the love in a friendship is philio. Love towards God, towards Theos (Theos is Greek for God) is agape. Love towards a spouse is yet another word.

In Greek, the definitions for these various words describing love are vastly different, and the words are much more specific, leaving less room for confusion. I mentioned much earlier in chapter 28, "Love", that on one very fraught occasion, my foster children wanted to know how they were loved. Did we love them less than we loved our birth children? I guess their question demonstrated how important love is.

I also mentioned in the previous chapter a great YouTube video, *The Power of One Caring Adult* (https://www.youtube.com/watch?v=u_Oapo1Q7_w). This video is all about dedicated time. But what *is* dedicated time? It seems to me that we dedicate time to things that are important to us—maybe even things or people that we love?

We do have a problem, I believe, in that we so deeply regard love solely as an emotion—which of course it is. However, I want to argue that it is also an act of one's will. What do I mean by that? I mean that we choose to love. The problem with our emotions is that they can often lead us all over the place. I think that, if you see a person whose life is governed by emotions, you are looking at a person who is in all sorts of life messes. Emotions are not good things to make life decisions on. Yes, I know that some people say the opposite. I assert that I think they are totally wrong. My own personal life experiences tell me I am right.

So, what am I making a plea for? I am making a plea for people to understand that there are many times that, by an act of our will, we choose to love. I know that, when people do that, their emotions should eventually come into synchronisation and fall into line with the action choice of our will.

Does that mean I love the wrong things that children do, be they birth children or foster children? No! Not at all! It does not mean that in any way. And it is not an easy thing to separate an action of the loved person from the person him or herself. I like the line in that YouTube video, where the foster carer says to the child, "We do not see you as a problem." That means that the actions people take are a problem, but the people themselves who perform the action are a separate issue. If one can change the thinking of the person concerned, then the person ceases to be problematical and, thereafter, becomes a success.

So unconditional love is that kind of love that continues to love, even when the person's actions are totally unacceptable. I like the words that the Bible tells us in the book of Romans. It really says two things. First, God does not like sin and regards us as sinners. Second, no matter how much He hates the sin, He nevertheless loves us and does not wait for us to change before he loves us.

It's a hard one. However, we must love the children put into our care as foster carers, even though many times we do not love what they are doing. Nevertheless, we keep on loving them as an act of our will, which ultimately will affect change in their thinking and, thus, alter their actions, leading to their greater possibility of life success.

CHAPTER FORTY-SEVEN

LISTENING

Someone said, "We have only one mouth but two ears, which probably means that we should listen more than we talk." One of the things I'm very aware of in the context of foster care is the need to listen to the children. I am *not* saying I always got it right. I *am* saying I knew it should be done.

As I have already said, we are blessed in my house in that we have two very spacious lounges. One of them I call the "noisy lounge." In this noisy room, there is a piano and a TV. That, to me, makes it the noisy room. The other room has sofas too. It also has an old-fashioned record player, because—did you know?—vinyl records are making a comeback. I refer to that lounge as the "quiet room". I noted that our foster children gave this room other names, such as "the museum". We like some old pictures that are in the quiet room, and I have already mentioned the "old" style record player. They, that is, the foster children, also referred to it as "the talking room".

It is true that we often used the quiet room as a place to sit and talk and, of course, to talk things through with our foster children from time to time. I had to laugh when I heard one child telling another—who the child thought had done something wrong—that if they were not careful, they would get called into the talking room.

For all the funny names, and the sometimes funny comments about the room, as foster carers, we found this talking room most helpful. To sit on a comfy chair, maybe even lounge a little and to talk, but also to really listen, was extremely useful. As a foster carer, it was incredibly helpful. Often in such situations, we tend to be not really listening but thinking about what we will say. Listening is a skill that we can learn. Could you, for example, repeat back to somebody what he or she has just told you, if you had to?

Not only did using this room for sharing purposes increase our understanding, it also often increased the child's perceptions of what was going on, and that was huge. When one articulates something to someone else, it really does help a person to sort out his or her own thinking. The process often gives the person a different perspective on what they're saying. Now, that is interesting, isn't it?

The biggest thing, however, is that the listening and the talking was often a great diffuser to what were, sometimes, extremely difficult situations. A situation that one must resist *always* (and one that foster carers may find themselves in often) is one in which the people involved are shouting *to* or *at* each other. The perfectly natural response is to want to shout back. When that takes place, though, all that happens is that everyone has damaged eardrums. And whatever the issue was that needed to be discussed merely remains at the status quo that the discussion started with. Or more likely, it has escalated and gotten worse.

I have experimented in classroom situations with large groups of children who are just being boisterous and making a lot of noise. If you stand close to such a group and speak very quietly about what you want to happen, very quickly, the whole group starts to shut up and listen. I suppose that it's the fear of missing out syndrome. He is talking, and I can't hear. Let me be quiet and listen. I find that, often the children will quieten and hush their friends too.

I mentioned a story in chapter 29, "Is Your Own Angst Hanging Out?" A social worker had come to our house and started shouting at our placement, who had said nothing and done nothing wrong. The way my wife handled the moment, and the manner in which my astute placement diffused it, was simply to listen and say nothing.

We then quietly moved into the quiet room ("the talking room", that is), where the social worker wound down. We all sat quietly in the room for a short while and then listened to her explain the reason for her visit. We politely answered his questions and finished the meeting. But then, as I said previously, my wife asked my placement to leave us alone and let us and the social worker do the talking.

Talk we did. My wife did not shout but firmly said, "Don't you dare talk to my very good young foster child like that ever again. You do not know her story. You have not read her files."

An apology followed from the social worker and an explanation about previous bad experiences with other children of a similar age. Fine! However, it should not have happened.

CHAPTER FORTY-EIGHT

LAC REVIEWS

When it comes to LAC reviews (looked after children reviews), there are many types of meetings that take place. Often the children will be told, "This meeting is for you. We want to hear your view. We want you to tell us what you think." I am sure that officialdom means what they say. The reality is, however, that, from many children's point of view, the truth of what takes place is completely different.

I have sat in the odd meeting (in other words, an LAC review) with some children who were very confident and extremely articulate. However, I have to say that those times are few and far between.

Remembering some meetings that I have been to with children who were placed with us, I am sure I would have felt intimidated were I in their place. I have sat in some with the child (that is, our placement); my wife and me; our supervising social worker and the child's social worker; a representative from the school and a representative from the police; an ad litem; and an independent chairperson. And in that officious and seriously legal setting, I have seen my placed child sit there in a hoodie with earphones on inside the hood giving great regard to what the floor looks like. Oh dear!

Then someone asks, "How are you? What's going on in your life? What do you want to say to this meeting, which has, of course, been called for your benefit?"

Talk about intimidation!

> If a child is made to feel intimidated, we are, in practise, clearly not achieving the desire to place the child at the centre of proceedings.

As I have said, I could conceivably be afraid of speaking in such a powerful august body. Now, I know that it is probably meant well, but I have often sat in such meetings feeling sorry for my child. I believe there must be a better, less intimidating way of getting a child's opinion or of running such a meeting.

Another thing that happens before reviews and meetings like this is that, at least once a year, there is a "review process". That is a review of the foster carer. Often, children are given a so-called "child-friendly form". They are requested to fill in this form that is asking them what they think about their carers, their lives, their school, and life in general. Simple! Often, as a foster carer, it has been my responsibility to give the said form to my foster child and say, "Could you fill this form in for the social worker please?" However, I must laugh when some of the children have come back to me saying, "Please, Adrian, could you tell me what to put on this form?"

Constantly, as a carer, I am told that the child is at the centre of all we do. This principle, policy, and/or paradigm is perfectly sound. So all parties concerned must constantly hold this mantra as the opening statement to any policy or practise. Yes, indeed. I totally agree with the sentiment and spirit of the statement.

However, it does worry me that some of our actions and our meeting processes, whilst they pay lip service to the "child-central philosophy, do not actually express that principle in practise.

I do not think that making a child feel intimidated and small or causing him or her to want to sit in a hoody with headphones on looking at the floor is, in practise, achieving the desire to place the child at the centre of proceedings. No matter how strongly the policy is verbally asserted, in practise, the opposite often actually takes place.

Of course, we need the views of the children. However, maybe we need to be more creative in getting those views. Maybe taking them out for an ice cream would work better. The ice cream would help rid the review of its officiousness.

CHAPTER FORTY-NINE

LEAVING CARE

Having discussed the trauma of a foster carer's beloved placement leaving his or her home home (chapter 43), we now briefly glance at the trauma of a foster child leaving the care system.

Just the word "leaving" is emotive and emotional. In the looked after system, leaving is one of those things that both children and foster carers must get used to. From my experience, it is always some kind of emotional roller coaster.

When a child moves from one placement to another, it can be for all sorts of reasons. We had one child placed with us because the previous foster carer had died. There had to be lots of emotion there.

One of the things that have annoyed me when I've collected children who are being placed in our care is finding that, in some places, all the child's belongings are being put in my car in black plastic bags. It feels to me that all the child's possessions are being thrown out. The first thing I do is to make sure that my foster care child has his or her own suitcase. It's a small thing I guess, but these small things make all sorts of impressions. Treasured possessions stuffed in a black plastic bag cannot seriously trigger anything but a negative response and impact on one's self-worth.

I am so glad that the government, bowing to pressure from various foster care agencies, have changed the rule that stated that children left care at 18. What used to happen was that, on the occasion of the eighteenth birthday, a child was moved to his or her own accommodation. Foster care just ceased. How crazy was that? Is it conceivable that one would do that to a birth child? I seriously hope not. Neither should it ever have happened to foster children.

Sometimes, social services will, sadly, put foster carers under emotional pressure, or should I say, blackmail. We certainly experienced it. A child who had been placed with us reached the grand old age of eighteen. From our point of view, she definitely was not ready to leave home. Along came the department saying, "Well, now she's eighteen; it's time for her to move on."

We responded and explained that we did not believe that should happen.

"OK," they said, "we'll let her stay, but you'll have to accept reduced remuneration. We can only fund to the level of a 'leaving care' placement, and that is much less than your 'foster care allowance'."

Oh dear! What would you have done?

We said, "So be it! The young lady is more important than the funding. However, we're not sure how we'll manage for all the things that she needs."

The rules now, I believe, are that, if the young person is in full-time education, he or she can stay in the foster care placement much longer. The problem is one of trying to put all children into the same box. I fostered one young girl who, at thirteen, would have coped perfectly well in her own accommodation. I hasten to add that she didn't have to. The other side of the coin is that we fostered another child until she had passed her nineteenth birthday, and she still found moving on to independence very difficult and needed lots of support.

Another "leaving process" that takes place is when a young person, at 16 years of age, moves from the social services family placement team, which deals with foster children generally, to the responsibility of the social services leaving care team. It's a case of different social workers, different managers, and different everyone and everything. I suppose one could just shrug one's shoulders and say, "Ah well! C'est la vie! That's life." However, the big thing I know is that young people in the LAC system desperately need stability, and each time these big changes take place, it's not easy and makes life an even greater challenge.

I think I mentioned earlier that it seems the worst kind of leaving is when a child leaves for adoption. And so that baby that has sort of been "yours" for so long is now gone.

Because social work is a kind of career-structured occupation, many social workers move from one local authority to another local authority to advance their careers or for better pay and conditions. The problem for the foster carer is having to deal with a child who, yet again, is faced with the *leaving* word. This raises an issue that is not easy to answer or resolve. However, we need to think about these things and about the children and carers facing the leaving.

CHAPTER FIFTY

EXTENDED FAMILY

This is my final foster care story that I have wanted to tell you about. I hope reading the stories has been a fun, interesting, and informative experience for you. Even more than that, I want to push for change in certain areas of the system in order to make it better. Remember, as I have already said, the worst enemy of better is very good.

This time, I want to go right back to the beginning. I'll tell you about my original assessment as a foster carer and one of the reasons I believe the local authority took so long to assess us.

The big issue, I think, is that we live in boxes; at least our thinking definitely does, anyway. What I mean about thinking in boxes and how that plays out practically can be summed up in the statement: "This is the way we have always done things, so this is the way we will always do them." Why try to fix what is already working? Woe betide anybody who we even perceive as wanting to deviate from the norm—even if the change he or she wants is better than the status quo.

You need to know that I'm not a native of London. I moved to the capital in 1974. I understood very quickly that there were lots of people who were struggling to find accommodation. I also understood very quickly that, for singles, living in a box by oneself can be somewhat depressing. TVs, Facebook, and iPhones are not the most positive alternative to somebody with skin on.

> If we exclude people from fostering because they cannot be squeezed into our mind box of what a "preferred family structure" is, that is not a good thing.

So, trying to think out of the box, we did something that was somewhat alternative and unconventional. We bought a very big house. It had six bedrooms, two lounges, three bathrooms, a kitchen, and a dining room. I could only afford a mortgage on this kind of house in London because of what I did, which was to start what I have named an "extended family home".

We had single friends around us in our community who needed places to live. And they did not really want to live alone. They were working in London. However, if you know London at all, you'll be aware that finding a pad is not always that easy. And so we embarked on this new concept. What we did was to invite these people to live with us. In our big house, we could have at least five people living there, plus us. I need to also add that, in those early years, we had three young children as well. We agreed that we would ask all our lodgers to contribute financially to our family budget, along with a request that, at least once a week, we all shared a family meal with everybody sat around the same table. We made it only a once a week thing, because we all had different times of coming home from work and going out and so on. It did make for a busy kitchen. and it did make for lots of work for my wife. People really did not like my cooking. I have never understood why.

Eventually, we made a deal with a local Chinese restaurant for Sunday lunches. The restaurant didn't normally open for Sunday lunch, but we made a deal with them for our exclusive use. Another problem arose when the Sunday family meal became so popular that our singles were bringing their boyfriends and girlfriends or just other friends for dinner too. It developed into a cooking and seating nightmare. The experiment proved so good and effective that we helped another family to do the same thing in another big house.

The problem was that planners decided that we needed to register as … something. So I suggested that they register us, legally and officially, as an "extended family home". It was not acceptable to the local authorities, simply because their tick box form did not have extended family home on its list. As I remember, I think they ticked the box that said "old person's home"—something we definitely were not.

So, when we agreed to become foster carers, oh dear!

"One cannot foster and have people living with them who are not one's related family."

"Why not?" I asked.

And here comes the oft-quoted statement. "Well! We haven't ever seen it before. We have nobody else that has ever done it."

It took a long time, but eventually, the burocrats succumbed, and we were registered. Our extended family was a great help in the fostering experience at our home. I need to add that the "family" had already been a great help to us in babysitting when our children were younger.

What we failed to remember is that our modern micro, or mini family, was a very new construct. The truth was that it is now "how people *used* to live". We think it's normal, but today it's not. It used to be. Many other cultures living in the United Kingdom still operate a different family setting and structure. Most Asian families would never dream of getting married and leaving home. They just extend the house and the senior person's home. In that culture, leaving home is not required, needed, or even entertained. The family takes care of and is committed to each other. That is normal living in that culture. And if we exclude people from fostering because they can't be squeezed into our mind box of what is a "preferred family structure", that is not a good thing.

There are many areas of fostering that I think are very good. However, that does not mean that some areas could not be done differently or, dare I say, better. It might mean different kinds of family structures. I have taken the trouble to look at models from other countries and their systems of caring for children. Some of them are quite different to how we do it in the United Kingdom. There are some good ideas out there. We are very foolish if we have closed minds, locked in "boxed thinking". Thinking that says, *This is the only way to do it,* is a serious error. There are many "hard to place children" out there. They are hard to place for all sorts of reasons—reasons, maybe, that need some new thinking.

It simply won't happen if our placement managers and our social workers all come from the same "Jobsworth" family or have been so conditioned by the system that they really believe there is no other way than their box.

Let's experiment. And let's make good even better.

CHAPTER FIFTY-ONE

DOES ANYTHING GO IN?

Good foster carers want to give to their placements much more than a roof over their heads, clothing, food, and water. At least I hope they do. I know that I did.

I wanted to put into a placement child good values and hopefully some self-confidence. I wanted to encourage the children we fostered to be successful adults. And by that, I mean able to be self-sufficient. I wanted them to growing into mature adults who could not only look after themselves well but also, as a sign of real maturity, look after others and, in fact, contribute positively to the world at large.

I must admit that there were many times I wondered if anything we were doing was "going in" or making any difference. Sure, the children were warm and fed and had a roof. But what was really going on inside them?

Now, many years on, I have had the privilege of seeing some of their successes. Sometimes what I see has been funny. One young lady, who introduced us as her parents, was a guest of honour at a very influential party with all the great and good of her society. We did get some very funny looks, being white and she being black. I think people wondered how we had managed that. Our once child placement did not bother to explain to the audience or the VIPs.

I listened to another young placement, now grown up, telling her friends how wonderful it had been living with her foster parents.

The foster home she spoke of sounded so idyllic that I wondered who lived in it and where it was. From what I earwigged of the story, there never seemed to be any problems whatsoever in the home. It was truly an amazing haven to be fostered in. Then I realised she was talking about her time with us. It's fascinating how time changes our perspectives. I certainly did not see all that happened when she lived with us in the same idyllic way that she did.

It's fascinating how time changes our perspectives.

Yet another time, I overheard a conversation on values with a past placement person. I often wondered if any of the values I had tried to communicate to this particular former foster child—values I believed would be good ones to put into her thinking—had found any resting place at all. In discussions with the young person while she was our placement, the absolute opposite would have been the disruptive position taken—totally opposite to my values, that is. Now I listened. My jaw almost dropped open as this older version of the same person propounded good life values that I thought had made no impact on her whatsoever. To say I was both encouraged and pleased is to put it mildly.

Finally, I'll share another situation with yet another young lady who had been placed with us. This time I was in conversation with a now much older but still young lady, who said to me, "You were so fortunate to have me as your foster child."

Of course! Who could disagree with such a statement? However, I did ask why she had come to that conclusion. Her answer amazed me so much that I, fortunately, was speechless.

Her reply was, "Well, you never had any 'teenage', problems with me. I never went through that awkward teenage stage that many others go through!"

Yet again I say, often with a sense of wonder, that it's amazing how differently two people can see things! But never mind. I offered heartfelt thanks, feeling glad that she felt that way. I certainly did not.

So, what am I saying? I am saying that the story is not over when the child leaves the responsibility of each foster carer. If, hopefully, you are or you want to be a foster carer and wonder what good you have done, once a child moves on, maybe you will receive the most wonderful privilege of seeing that person years later. However, it must be added that you just might have to wait for that wonderful moment. Be encouraged. Some of those good things you are sharing are definitely "going in".

ABOUT THE AUTHOR

Adrian Hawkes

A native of Birmingham, United Kingdom, Adrian Hawkes's first daytime job was in the fashion trade. His evening activity was leading a team of young people running youth events around the city and, ultimately, in the very centre of Birmingham. This team of four led more than a hundred young people. Every Sunday night at 9 p.m., their youth events brought hundreds of young people together.

Moving on after many lucrative years in the rag trade, Adrian worked for six months in Port Talbot, Wales, helping to establish a church there. From that experience, Adrian believed he should train in theology and received his training at Capel College, Surrey, England.

After training, Adrian was posted in the North East of England. He was there for five years, getting married a week into the job. Adrian was then posted to North London to take charge of two separate church communities. By this time, he was part of a small family community himself, having not only a wife but also two small children.

Forty-seven years on, London is still his home. The church community he worked with grew to many hundreds. He then reached out, establishing independent sector schools and nurseries, housing, and work for the unemployed. At one stage, the church employed more than three hundred people.

Adrian is on the board of several companies and involved in all sorts of activities, all for social good.

He travels extensively, working and advising groups in Switzerland, Sri Lanka, Germany, Canada, and France. He is also on the trust of a community in the United States of America.

Adrian has been invited to speak at the United Nations on the need to do something positive for refugees and displaced persons worldwide.

Following a traumatic experience with one young person in particular, Adrian and his wife, Pauline, decided they needed to understand such youth and how to effectively help them. They signed up to a local authority training course. The training displayed the contemporary need for foster carers. It was a no-brainer as far as they were concerned. They fostered for over fifteen years, fostering emergency cases of over thirty young people over those years. *I Was a Foster Carer* tells of some of the stories they experienced at that time.

Adrian has sometimes amalgamated stories in the book to make his point. However, please note that every story told, no matter how strange you think it is, actually and factually took place.

I Was a Foster Carer asks, Could you be a foster carer?

I hope you will enjoy the read. Please do comment by blog, Twitter, or email. Or write to the publisher, who will forward it on.

Other books by Adrian Hawkes

- *Leadership and …* (on its third print with about 18,000 in circulation)
  - Spanish edition, *Lidezago y …*
- *Jacob: A Fatherless Generation*
  - Spanish edition, *Jacob: Una Generación Huéfana*
- *Hello, Is That You God?*
- *Attracting Training Releasing Youth* (on its second print with 12,000 copies in circulation)
  - Spanish edition, *Atrayendo, Entrenando y Enviando Jóvenes*
- *Culture Clash*
  - Spanish edition, *Choqui de Culturas*
- *Icejacked* (a fiction book)
  - Spanish edition, *Congelado*
- *Perspectives: The Alphabet of Life*

Blog addresses for Adrian Hawkes

- http://adrianhawkes.blogspot.co.uk/
- http://adrianhawkes.co.uk/
- https://adrian2526.wordpress.com/
- http://adriansspanishblog.blogspot.co.uk/

Printed in the United States
by Baker & Taylor Publisher Services